The Harcourt Brace Casebook Series in Literature

"A Rose for Emily"

William Faulkner

The Harcourt Brace Casebook Series in Literature
Series Editors: Laurie G. Kirszner and Stephen R. Mandell

"A Rose for Emily"

William Faulkner

Contributing Editor

Noel Polk
University of Southern Mississippi

Harcourt College Publishers

Fort Worth   Philadelphia   San Diego   New York   Orlando   Austin   San Antonio
Toronto   Montreal   London   Sydney   Tokyo

Publisher	Earl McPeek
Acquisitions Editor	Bill Hoffman
Project Editor	Christy Goldfinch
Art Director	Vicki Whistler
Production Manager	Linda McMillan

ISBN: 0-15-507471-7

Library of Congress Catalog Card Number: 99-068267

Copyright © 2000 by Harcourt, Inc.

Harcourt College Publishers will provide complimentary supplements or supplement packages to those adopters qualified under our adoption policy. Please contact your sales representative to learn how you qualify. If as an adopter or potential user you receive supplements you do not need, please return them to your sales representative or send them to: Attn: Returns Department, Troy Warehouse, 465 South Lincoln Drive, Troy, MO 63379.

Address for Domestic Orders
Harcourt, Inc., 6277 Sea Harbor Drive, Orlando, FL 32887-6777
800-782-4479

Address for International Orders
International Customer Service
Harcourt, Inc., 6277 Sea Harbor Drive, Orlando, FL 32887-6777
407-345-3800
(fax) 407-345-4060
(e-mail) hbintl@harcourtbrace.com

Address for Editorial Correspondence
Harcourt, Inc., 301 Commerce Street, Suite 3700, Fort Worth, TX 76102

Web Site Address
http://www.harcourtcollege.com

Printed in the United States of America

9 0 1 2 3 4 5 6 7 8   066   9 8 7 6 5 4 3 2 1

Harcourt College Publishers

THE HARCOURT BRACE CASEBOOK SERIES IN LITERATURE
Series Editors: Laurie G. Kirszner and Stephen R. Mandell

DRAMA
Athol Fugard
"Master Harold" . . . *and the boys*

William Shakespeare
Hamlet

POETRY
Emily Dickinson
A Collection of Poems

Langston Hughes
A Collection of Poems

Walt Whitman
A Collection of Poems

FICTION
William Faulkner
"A Rose for Emily"

Charlotte Perkins Gilman
"The Yellow Wallpaper"

Flannery O'Connor
"A Good Man Is Hard to Find"

John Updike
"A&P"

Eudora Welty
"A Worn Path"

ABOUT THE SERIES

The Harcourt Casebook Series in Literature has its origins in our anthology *Literature: Reading, Reacting, Writing* (Third Edition, 1997), which in turn arose out of our many years of teaching college writing and literature courses. The primary purpose of each Casebook in the series is to offer students a convenient, self-contained reference tool that they can use to complete a research project for an introductory literature course.

In choosing subjects for the Casebooks, we draw on our own experience in the classroom, selecting works of poetry, fiction, and drama that students like to read, discuss, and write about and that teachers like to teach. Unlike other collections of literary criticism aimed at student audiences, the Harcourt Casebook Series in Literature features short stories, groups of poems, or plays (rather than longer works, such as novels) because these are the genres most often taught in college-level Introduction to Literature courses. In selecting particular authors and titles, we focus on those most popular with students and those most accessible to them.

To facilitate student research—and to facilitate instructor supervision of that research—each casebook contains all the resources students need to produce a documented research paper on a particular work of literature. Every casebook in the series includes the following elements:

- A comprehensive **introduction** to the work, providing social, historical, and political background. This introduction helps students to understand the work and the author in the context of a particular time and place. In particular, the introduction enables students to appreciate customs, situations, and events that may have contributed to the author's choice of subject matter, emphasis, or style.

- A **headnote,** including birth and death dates of the author; details of the work's first publication and its subsequent publication history, if relevant; details about the author's life; a summary of the author's career; and a list of key published works, with dates of publication.

- The most widely accepted version of the **literary work,** along with the explanatory footnotes students will need to understand unfamiliar terms and concepts or references to people, places, or events.

- **Discussion questions** focusing on themes developed in the work. These questions, designed to stimulate critical thinking and discussion, can also serve as springboards for research projects.

- Several extended **research assignments** related to the literary work. Students may use these assignments exactly as they appear in the Casebook, or students or instructors may modify the assignments to suit their own needs or research interests.

- A diverse collection of traditional and nontraditional **secondary sources,** which may include scholarly articles, reviews, interviews, memoirs, newspaper articles, historical documents, and so on. This resource offers students access to sources they might not turn to on their own — for example, a popular song that inspired a short story, a story that was the original version of a play, a legal document that sheds light on a work's theme, or two different biographies of an author — thus encouraging students to look beyond the obvious or the familiar as they search for ideas. Students may use only these sources, or they may supplement them with sources listed in the Casebook's bibliography (see below).

- An annotated model **student research paper** drawing on several of the casebook's secondary sources. This paper uses MLA parenthetical documentation and includes a Works Cited list conforming to MLA style.

- A comprehensive **bibliography** of print and electronic sources related to the work. This bibliography offers students an opportunity to move beyond the sources in the Casebook to other sources related to a particular research topic.

- A concise **guide to MLA documentation,** including information on what kinds of information require documentation (and what kinds do not); a full explanation of how to construct parenthetical references and how to place them in a paper; sample parenthetical reference formats for various kinds of sources used in papers about literature; a complete explanation of how to assemble a list of Works Cited, accompanied by sample works cited entries (including formats for documenting electronic sources); and guidelines for using explanatory notes (with examples).

By collecting all this essential information in one convenient place, each volume in the Harcourt Casebook Series in Literature responds to the needs of both students and teachers. For students, the casebooks offer convenience, referentiality, and portability that make the process of doing research easier. Thus the Casebooks recognize what students already know: that Introduction to Literature is not their only class and the literature research paper is not their only assignment. For instructors, the casebooks offer a rare combination of flexibility and control in the classroom. For example, teachers may choose to assign one casebook or more than one; thus, they have the option of having all students in a class write about the same work or having different groups of students, or individual students, write about different works. In addition, instructors may ask students to use only the secondary sources collected in the casebook, thereby controlling students' use of (and acknowledgment of) sources more closely, or they may encourage students to seek both print and electronic sources beyond those included in the casebook. By building convenience, structure, and flexibility into each volume, we have designed The Harcourt Casebook Series in Literature to suit a wide variety of teaching styles and research interests. The casebooks have made the research paper an easier project for us and a less stressful one for our students; we hope they will do the same for you.

Laurie G. Kirszner
Stephen R. Mandell
Series Editors

PREFACE

"A Rose for Emily," one of William Faulkner's earliest published stories, is one of his most often anthologized pieces of fiction, and the one with which he is most often identified by readers who encounter his work in surveys of literature in high school and college, and who take it to be "typical" of his work. In most ways this identification is not quite fair because from one perspective "A Rose for Emily" is by no means typical of his work. However, it is in many other ways so replete with themes and issues he tackled throughout his fiction, from beginning to end, that many scholars consider it an important entry into his fictional world.

Although set in and against the backdrop of Faulkner's very traditional antebellum Southern town, Jefferson (the fictional county seat of his fictional Yoknapatawpha County), "A Rose for Emily" is by no means a traditional "Southern" story. It is rather a study of personality traits and family dynamics that Sigmund Freud's work forced on the consciousness of the modern world. The story thus combines a traditional setting with modern psychology in ways that revolutionized the genre of the "Southern Gothic" and, in effect, demonstrated just how modern the South was. In any case, it is by almost universal consent among scholars, critics, and informed readers one of the twentieth century's great masterpieces in the short story form.

The articles collected in this volume explore various aspects of the story's narrative, its psychological complexities, its characterization, and its themes. They are designed not merely to give you easy access to what others have had to say about this remarkable piece of fiction, but also to help you learn how to form your own critical judgments of the story. Here is a list of the secondary sources.

- Faulkner's responses to students' questions about the story at the University of Virginia during his time as writer in residence.

- Terry Heller, "The Telltale Hair: A Critical Study of William Faulkner's 'A Rose for Emily.'" Heller's commentary offers a good overview of the story's narrative and themes.
- George L. Dillon, "Styles of Reading." Using "A Rose for Emily" as his example, Dillon demonstrates how readers respond to a work of literature according to what they are looking for when they read.
- Robert Crosman, "How Readers Make Meaning." Crosman suggests how readers bring to their reading their own sets of experiences and aesthetic and life principles that help determine what they take the meaning of an individual work of literature to be.
- Ruth Sullivan, "The Narrator in 'A Rose for Emily.'" Sullivan discusses not just conventional "point of view" in the story, but also the narrator's complicity in the story he is telling.
- Isaac Rodman, "Irony and Isolation: Narrative Distance in Faulkner's 'A Rose for Emily.'" Rodman takes issue with the critical consensus that the narrator speaks for the community of Jefferson and argues he is in most ways as isolated from the community as Emily is herself.
- Suzanne Hunter Brown, "'A Rose for Emily,' by William Faulkner." Brown reflects on the differences between the "sequential" manner in which Emily's life in Jefferson occurred and the "configurational" manner in which the narrator reports it.
- Jack Scherting, "Emily Grierson's Oedipus Complex: Motif, Motive, and Meaning in Faulkner's 'A Rose for Emily.'" The author explores Faulkner's story through Freudian psychoanalysis.
- Judith Fetterley, "A Rose for 'A Rose for Emily.'" Fetterley's feminist reading asks readers to consider the patriarchal assumptions behind the town's and the narrator's attitudes toward Emily's life and death.
- Gene M. Moore, "Of Time and Its Mathematical Progression: Problems of Chronology in Faulkner's 'A Rose for Emily.'" Moore untangles the story's chronology by examining Faulkner's original manuscript.

Acknowledgments

I thank Laurie G. Kirszner and Stephen R. Mandell, editors of this series, for their most helpful comments as this volume was being prepared, and my Harcourt team: Bill Hoffman, acquisitions editor; Christy Goldfinch, project editor; Vicki Whistler, art director; Linda McMillan, production manager; and Kassandra Radomski, freelance editor. I also thank Michael Salda, chair of the English Department at the University of Southern Mississippi, for many favors and much assistance. Finally, I am grateful to my student assistant Liz Brister for all her hard work on the volume.

CONTENTS

Introduction

"A Rose for Emily": Faulkner's Modern Gothic Masterpiece

The year 1929, when William Faulkner wrote "A Rose for Emily," was one of the most eventful years in U.S. history. In literature it was *annus mirabilis,* a year of miracles that saw the publication of Ernest Hemingway's *A Farewell to Arms,* Thomas Wolfe's *Look Homeward Angel,* and Faulkner's first great novel, *The Sound and the Fury.* Economically, politically, and socially—and morally, many said—however, the country seemed headed toward collapse; indeed, the stock market's disastrous crash in October ushered in the beginning of the Great Depression of the thirties, a period of unparalleled poverty and discontent in the United States that caused many otherwise patriotic Americans to question the meaning of the "American Dream."

WORLD WAR AND DISILLUSION

In fact, the entire decade of the twenties had been a time of questioning of American and Western values. Indeed, it can be argued that the twenties actually began in the previous decade, during the First World War (1914–18). This war, which many call the first modern war, was heralded by politicians (and sold to the American public) as "the war to end all wars" and as the war that would "make the world safe for democracy." But World War I was actually a crucible in which traditional values were tested and found wanting. Young men who had gone into that war idealistically saw death and dismemberment on a scale previously unimaginable; it was a war fought not by heroes in hand-to-hand combat with an honorable enemy but rather by faceless, nameless soldiers who shot missiles and gas pellets and machine guns at unseen and equally nameless, faceless enemies. The trenches themselves became deathtraps: reservoirs of mud, rats, and disease that killed as many soldiers as artillery did. Not much was honorable about such combat. Soldiers on both sides returned, as Vietnam veterans did two or three generations later, disillusioned with the idealism and the political jargon that had sent them to such a hell. Poet Ezra Pound aptly summed up the sense of the age in his "Hugh Selwyn Mauberly":

These fought in any case,
And some believing,
            Pro domo in any case . . .
Some quick to arm,
some for adventure,
some from fear of weakness,
some from fear of censure,
some for love of slaughter, in imagination,
learning later . . .
some in fear, learning love of slaughter;
Died some, pro patria,
            non "dulce" non "et décor" . . .
walked eye-deep in hell
believing in old men's lies, then unbelieving
came home, home to a lie,
home to many deceits,
home to old lies and new infamy;
usury age-old and age-thick
and liars in public places.
Daring as never before, wastage as never before.
Young blood and high blood,
fair cheeks, and fine bodies;
fortitude as never before
frankness as never before,
disillusions as never told in the old days,
hysterias, trench confessions,
laughter out of dead bellies.
  . . .
There died a myriad,
And of the best, among them,
For an old bitch gone in the teeth,
For a botched civilization,

Charm, smiling at the good mouth,
Quick eyes gone under earth's lid,

For two gross of broken statues,
For a few thousand battered books.

Soldiers came home to disillusionment—or rather, brought it home with them. The literature of the period registers their cynicism about all the abstractions that characterized political and social discourse, about abstract ideals such as patriotism and democracy. Writers on both sides of the conflict wrote remarkable and graphic stories and novels about the times. Erich Maria Remarque's best-selling novel *All Quiet on the Western Front* (1929), for example, depicts the horrors of the actual battlefield from the German point of view. American writers, however, seemed more concerned with the social and cultural upheaval following the war when soldiers, attempting to repatriate themselves, found the homes they had left completely and irrevocably altered upon their return. Ernest Hemingway's powerful short story "Soldier's Home," for example, suggests the degree to which the experience of war had alienated young men of his generation from the comforts of home, family, and country. Little wonder, then, that many Americans, the ones who could afford it, fled from home to try to find themselves.

PROSPERITY, PSYCHOLOGY, MOBILITY, AND THE JAZZ AGE

Many Americans fled on new highways in their new automobiles, which in the booming postwar economy became available at low cost. By 1929, one fifth of Americans owned automobiles, and this cheap mobility helped foster the internal upheaval that went on during the twenties. Others moved from rural to urban environments seeking new and better jobs: an increasing number of southern blacks, for example, escaped their sharecropper lives by moving to Detroit, Chicago, New York, and other northern cities. Still others fled from what they considered the repressive morality of Prohibition America to bootleggers' establishments to party their cares away or to Europe, particularly to Paris, whose postwar economy, in shambles for years, made it easy for Americans with even meager amounts of American dollars to live very well. Paris's more relaxed attitudes about sex and alcohol made it particularly attractive to the large expatriate community.

F. Scott Fitzgerald depicted the twenties, commonly referred to as the "Jazz Age," in his stories and novels (especially *The Great Gatsby,* 1925, and *Tender Is the Night,* 1934) as an era of incredible wealth and conspicuous consumption. And although modern historians now believe the excesses of the Jazz Age have been somewhat exaggerated, it is clear that writers took the postwar excesses seriously: while depicting those excesses, they were also weighing their spiritual costs. Gertrude Stein told Hemingway that his was a "lost generation," a phrase he made famous when he used it as one of the epigraphs to *The Sun Also Rises,* his novel about expatriates in a spin of sex and alcohol and frustration in Paris and Spain. Fitzgerald's *Tender Is the Night* chronicles Dick Diver's seduction and eventual destruction by the power of money and the people who control it.

But it was not just the war, physical mobility, and wealth that defined the age. Women, granted the right to vote in 1919, began to express other forms of freedom—in the way they dressed, in their social behavior, and in their sexual attitudes. The twenties, the Jazz Age, was also the era of the "flapper," that bobbed-haired, Charleston-dancing, cigarette-smoking symbol of America's escape from Victorian sexual repression.

At the same time, the writings of Sigmund Freud, the great Viennese neurologist and founder of psychoanalysis, gave people access to the human unconscious—that vast reservoir of memory wherein, according to Freud, we bury our earliest experiences of shame, childhood terror, and sexual repression, the dark places where our nightmares and our neuroses begin. Serious thinkers, especially novelists, found in Freud a revolutionary way to understand character: the idea of the unconscious provided them with a hugely expanded capacity to suggest motives for otherwise irrational acts. The popularized version of Freud's writings, or at least the part of his ideas that filtered into the culture at large, emphasized the extent to which sexual repression at an early age creates unhealthy adults. "Freud" thus became a kind of justification for any kind of sexual or expressive excess, and many did exactly what they wanted, claiming to be escaping from repression.

Finally, in Russia, the Bolsheviks had wrested power from the czars in 1917, and conservatives in America feared that communism had been loosed on the world. Economic disruptions caused by strikes in the U.S. work force were blamed on the developing communist menace.

Conservative forces were quick to confront these forces of revolution. Hard on the heels of women's winning the right to vote in 1919, for example, the Miss America pageant was created, implicitly to provide American women with "correct" ideas about how a modern American woman was to comport herself. Two Italian immigrants, Nicola Sacco and Bartolomeo Vanzetti, were executed in 1927 for a murder the evidence suggested they did not commit—punished, many believed, for their anarchist principles. Religious fervor, sweeping the land in revivals led by Billy Sunday and Aimee Semple McPherson, challenged the forces of modernism. In Tennessee, in the infamous Scopes "monkey" trial, teacher John Scopes was convicted of violating a state law when he dared to teach evolution in his high school classroom.

FAULKNER'S MODERNITY

Although William Faulkner traveled to Europe in the mid-twenties, he managed to remain aloof from the excesses of the Jazz Age. He spent about six months in France, mostly as an observer of the art and the customs, but he came home to ground himself in his native Mississippi. But he was by no means out of touch with cultural and intellectual currents in his own country and in Europe. "A Rose for Emily" may appear on first reading to be quite different from Fitzgerald's stories of the same period, and it is; but it too reflects those parts of the looming twentieth century that most interested Faulkner and other authors. At a basic level, for example, it could be argued that the story can happen precisely because of the increased mobility in American life described here: indeed, Emily's first lover, Homer Barron, comes to town to build sidewalks. More deeply, however, "A Rose for Emily" (as so many of the commentators, many collected here, have noted) is grounded in Freudian psychology, specifically in the Oedipus complex. Oxford, Mississippi, may have been in some ways a backwater, but Faulkner, its most famous citizen, was fully aware of the cultural and intellectual movements astir in the rest of the world.

"A Rose for Emily" was written in the late fall of 1929 and published in the literary magazine *Forum* in April 1930. It is among the most frequently anthologized short stories by an American author and among the most often studied stories in the American canon. It is the story with which William Faulkner is most often identified by the popular reading public. In fact, it is often the only Faulkner story that many college and high school students ever read. Readers find it difficult to forget the horror of the final scene, and thus carry with them throughout their lives a sense of Faulkner as a "shock" writer, a morbid man whose affinities for the grotesque and the bizarre place him in the company of Edgar Allan Poe and Stephen King rather than in the roster of writers like Shakespeare and Dickens. This is a curious and unfortunate fate for Faulkner's reputation, because "A Rose for Emily" is in many ways very *un*typical of Faulkner. Nowhere else, in fact, does he show any interest whatsoever in necrophilia, although to be sure throughout his fiction he explores the pathologies of morbidity, especially as they occur within the dynamics of family structures.

At the same time, however, "A Rose for Emily" is typical, even emblematic, of Faulkner's work: its geographical setting of Jefferson in north

Mississippi; its temporal placement within the larger context of southern history (even if here only hinted at); its analysis of the community; its interest in family dysfunction; and its concern with repressive patriarchal structures that warp sexuality, especially that of females.

Many of Faulkner's best-known characters are indeed obsessed with sex and death, like other characters in twentieth-century American fiction, and in this sense there is *not* (despite what some critics say) anything peculiarly "Southern" about the themes in "A Rose for Emily." Even so, the story has often been taken to be quintessentially Southern, thanks to Faulkner's almost complete identification as a "Southern" writer and to ongoing critical interest in his Southernness, both that traditional Southernness associated with Old South gentility and the more recent sort, focusing on a "fallen" and unreconstructed South that associates the region with racism, poverty, and faded gentility. Recent criticism, however, more interested in the story's modernity, has examined the Freudian dimensions in "A Rose for Emily," its language, and its narration, and has demonstrated its relevance to a whole range of gender and culture issues both in Faulkner and in American literature and culture generally.

THE MODERN GOTHIC

For better or worse, "A Rose for Emily" has come to define a whole subgenre of American fiction, the Southern Gothic. This term accepts the story's "Southernness" as a given and then imbues that Southernness with the strain of American Gothicism probably best exemplified by Poe's "The Fall of the House of Usher." It is not difficult to see how the Southern and the Gothic complement each other. Gothicism, of course, reaches far back into the beginnings of the novel itself and is especially indebted to British Romanticism and such novels as *The Castle of Otranto, Jane Eyre,* and *Wuthering Heights.* Two of the best-known American examples are Nathaniel Hawthorne's *The House of Seven Gables* and Faulkner's *Absalom, Absalom!* Gothic romances often take place in gloomy settings, in decaying castles or mansions in which characters, most often women, are trapped, dying, or doomed to suffer, or are threatened in one way or another by invisible and unexplained terrors. Quite often the terror heroines feel is a result of an ancestral "secret" of some sort, contained in and embodied by the house itself (with "house" meaning "family," as in the House of Usher). The plots of these novels move toward a disastrous climax, usually the revelation of that family secret—the ultimate horror. Authors used the gloom and foreboding, the decay and the sense of entrapment, as devices for exploring complex psychological and sexual problems that the language and conventions of the nineteenth century did not permit them to depict any more openly. The writings of Sigmund Freud in the twentieth century, of course, gave writers a brand-new language, the symbolic language of dreaming—psychoanalysis—that has allowed us to reread the Gothic masterpieces in an entirely modern light.

In "A Rose for Emily," Faulkner joins Freudian theory, particularly the Oedipus complex, to the Southern Gothic. But he turns that Gothic plot back in on itself: the trapped heroine here literally embraces the horror rather than shrinking from it or being terrified by it, and in so doing reveals the true horror—incest, real or imagined—at the secret heart of family itself. "A Rose for Emily," then, for all its traditional Southernness, is quintessentially modern.

WORKS CONSULTED

Fussell, Paul. *The Great War and Modern Memory.* New York: Oxford UP, 1975.

Hoffman, Frederick J. *The Twenties: American Writing in the Postwar Decade.* Rev. ed. New York: Free, 1962.

Horton, Rod W., and Herbert W. Edwards. *Backgrounds of American Literary Thought.* 3rd ed. Englewood Cliffs: Prentice, 1974.

Kennedy, J. Gerald. *Imagining Paris: Exile, Writing, and American Identity.* New Haven: Yale UP, 1993.

Kerr, Elizabeth. *William Faulkner's Gothic Domain.* Port Washington, NY: Kennikat, 1979.

Literature

About the Author

WILLIAM FAULKNER (1897–1962) was born in New Albany, Mississippi, and moved with his family to Oxford very soon thereafter. The great-grandson of a Confederate army officer, Faulkner was raised, at least partially, by Caroline Barr, a former family slave, who lived well into Faulkner's forties. Although he traveled extensively, he continued to live and work in Oxford for the rest of his life. In ways that most readers who visit Oxford can easily see, he modeled his fictional Yoknapatawpha County and its county seat, Jefferson, on Oxford's political and geographical layout—the square with the antebellum courthouse in its center—and drew on his region's and his family's history for a good deal of the fiction that critics consider his best.

These facts have encouraged many critics over the years to seek to understand Faulkner only as a Southerner, not as a preeminent modernist whose astonishing achievements in such novels as *The Sound and the Fury* (1929), *As I Lay Dying* (1930), *Sanctuary* (1931), *Light in August* (1932), *Absalom, Absalom!* (1936), *The Hamlet* (1940), and *Go Down, Moses* (1942) redefined the possibilities for the novel for the next several generations of writers. His influence on writers throughout the world, such as Albert Camus, Jorge Luis Borges, and Gabriel García Márquez, has been testified to by the writers themselves and demonstrated by legions of critics.

In 1918, Faulkner went to Canada, where he lied about his age in order to enlist in the Royal Air Force and fight in World War I, but the war's end shattered his dreams of becoming a pilot. He returned home to Oxford after his training, wore his uniform and affected a limp; he told his friends that he was wounded and had a metal plate in his head. Enrolling in the university, he became known as "Count No-Count" for his generally affected airs and his involvement with artistic and literary projects. He reviewed books for the student newspaper and he joined a drama club, The Marionettes, and helped stage several productions, even writing a one-act play for the group titled "The Marionettes." He read omnivorously throughout this period, as he did throughout his life. He had access to both the University of Mississippi library and the personal library of his friend and mentor, Yale graduate Phil Stone, a local lawyer, who bought books for himself and obligingly lent them to and discussed them with his young friend. Faulkner spent endless hours reading, writing, and revising poetry. Stone helped him finance the publication of his first book, *The Marble Faun,* a slender volume containing a cycle of poems that appeared in 1924.

But Faulkner soon grew tired of life in Oxford and headed for Europe, like so many other young Americans in the twenties. In January 1925 he went to New Orleans, hoping to earn enough money to pay for a cheap passage across the Atlantic, but there he met Sherwood Anderson, one of America's leading literary figures at that time, and a variety of other aesthetes living and working in the French Quarter. Here he continued to read and write and talked with his new friends about all the current literary gossip. He wrote his first novel, *Soldiers' Pay* (1926), in New Orleans, and he would make his second, *Mosquitoes* (1927), a *roman à clef* (literally, "a novel with a key"; that is, a novel keyed to characters in the real world) about his time there. On July 7, he finally sailed for Europe with his friend, the artist William Spratling, and spent six months abroad, most of that time in Paris, absorbing the culture and desolation of postwar Europe.

By the time he returned to Oxford in December, Faulkner had come to realize that he would make a more productive life for himself by living in Mississippi rather than in Europe and becoming an expatriate like Hemingway and Fitzgerald. He discovered his own *donnée,* his literary subject, in what he later claimed Sherwood Anderson told him was his "little postage stamp of native soil" in north Mississippi, and he spent the rest of his life creating a fictional world out of the history and traditions and topography of his native region. Most of his novels and stories take place in his mythical—he called it apocryphal—Yoknapatawpha County and its county seat of Jefferson, and he treated the people he created as citizens of a great community who appear in one novel or story and often reappear in minor or even more important roles in another. Yoknapatawpha County is a great sprawling cosmos, which, for all its "Southernness" of geography and history and culture, is a microcosm of all America.

Despite his base in Mississippi, however, Faulkner spent a good deal of time away from home. In the thirties and forties, because his novels and stories were not selling well enough for him to support his family, he worked off and on as a screenwriter in Hollywood; in the fifties, after the Nobel Prize had made him financially secure, he traveled to countries throughout the world as a cultural emissary for the U.S. State Department, reading from his work and answering questions about it. Also during the fifties, he emerged from his private life as an author to speak out about racial injustice in his native state and region. In a series of speeches and essays, he addressed the South's need to correct the economic, educational, and political injustices that black citizens in the South suffered. His outspoken views on racial matters made him less popular in his native state than he had ever been. Even so, during the last twelve years of his life he was one of the most honored and respected of American writers. Among many other prizes, he was awarded two Pulitzers, for *A Fable* (1954) and *The Reivers* (1962), and he received the Nobel Prize in 1950. Faulkner died in 1962.

WILLIAM FAULKNER

A Rose for Emily
(1930)

I

When Miss Emily Grierson died, our whole town went to her funeral: the men through a sort of respectful affection for a fallen monument, the women mostly out of curiosity to see the inside of her house, which no one save an old manservant—a combined gardener and cook—had seen in at least ten years.

It was a big, squarish frame house that had once been white, decorated with cupolas and spires and scrolled balconies in the heavily lightsome style of the seventies, set on what had once been our most select street. But garages and cotton gins had encroached and obliterated even the august names of that neighborhood; only Miss Emily's house was left, lifting its stubborn and coquettish decay above the cotton wagons and the gasoline pumps—an eyesore among eyesores. And now Miss Emily had gone to join the representatives of those august names where they lay in the cedar-bemused cemetery among the ranked and anonymous graves of Union and Confederate soldiers who fell at the battle of Jefferson.

Alive, Miss Emily had been a tradition, a duty, and a care; a sort of hereditary obligation upon the town, dating from that day in 1894 when Colonel Sartoris, the mayor—he who fathered the edict that no Negro woman should appear on the streets without an apron—remitted her taxes, the dispensation dating from the death of her father on into perpetuity. Not that Miss Emily would have accepted charity. Colonel Sartoris invented an involved tale to the effect that Miss Emily's father had loaned money to the town, which the town, as a matter of business, preferred this way of repaying. Only a man of Colonel Sartoris' generation and thought could have invented it, and only a woman could have believed it.

When the next generation, with its more modern ideas, became mayors and aldermen, this arrangement created some little dissatisfaction. On the first of the year they mailed her a tax notice. February came, and there was no reply. They wrote her a formal letter, asking her to call at the sheriff's office at her convenience. A week later the mayor wrote her himself, offering to call or to send his car for her, and received in reply a note on paper of an archaic shape, in a thin, flowing calligraphy in faded ink, to the effect that she no longer went out at all. The tax notice was also enclosed, without comment.

They called a special meeting of the Board of Aldermen. A deputation waited upon her, knocked at the door through which no visitor had passed since she ceased giving china-painting lessons eight or ten years earlier. They were admitted by the old Negro into a dim hall from which a stairway mounted into still more shadow. It smelled of dust and disuse—a close, dank smell. The Negro led them into the parlor. It was furnished in heavy, leather-covered furniture. When the Negro opened the blinds of one window, they could see that the leather was cracked; and when they sat down, a faint dust rose sluggishly about their thighs, spinning with slow motes in the single sun-ray. On a tarnished gilt easel before the fireplace stood a crayon portrait of Miss Emily's father.

They rose when she entered—a small, fat woman in black, with a thin gold chain descending to her waist and vanishing into her belt, leaning on an ebony cane with a tarnished gold head. Her skeleton was small and spare; perhaps that was why what would have been merely plumpness in another was obesity in her. She looked bloated, like a body long submerged in motionless water, and of that pallid hue. Her eyes, lost in the fatty ridges of her face, looked like two small pieces of coal pressed into a lump of dough as they moved from one face to another while the visitors stated their errand.

She did not ask them to sit. She just stood in the door and listened quietly until the spokesman came to a stumbling halt. Then they could hear the invisible watch ticking at the end of the gold chain.

Her voice was dry and cold. "I have no taxes in Jefferson. Colonel Sartoris explained it to me. Perhaps one of you can gain access to the city records and satisfy yourselves."

"But we have. We are the city authorities, Miss Emily. Didn't you get a notice from the sheriff, signed by him?"

"I received a paper, yes," Miss Emily said. "Perhaps he considers himself the sheriff . . . I have no taxes in Jefferson."

"But there is nothing on the books to show that, you see. We must go by the—"

"See Colonel Sartoris. I have no taxes in Jefferson."

"But, Miss Emily—"

"See Colonel Sartoris." (Colonel Sartoris had been dead almost ten years.) "I have no taxes in Jefferson. Tobe!" The Negro appeared. "Show these gentlemen out."

II

So she vanquished them, horse and foot, just as she had vanquished their fathers thirty years before about the smell. That was two years after her father's death and a short time after her sweetheart—the one we believed would marry her—had deserted her. After her father's death she went out very little; after her sweetheart went away, people hardly saw her at all. A few of the ladies had the temerity to call, but were not received, and the only sign of life about the place was the Negro man—a young man then—going in and out with a market basket.

"Just as if a man—any man—could keep a kitchen properly," the ladies said; so they were not surprised when the smell developed. It was another link between the gross, teeming world and the high and mighty Griersons.

A neighbor, a woman, complained to the mayor, Judge Stevens, eighty years old.

"But what will you have me do about it, madam?" he said.

"Why, send her word to stop it," the woman said. "Isn't there a law?"

"I'm sure that won't be necessary," Judge Stevens said. "It's probably just a snake or a rat that nigger of hers killed in the yard. I'll speak to him about it."

The next day he received two more complaints, one from a man who came in diffident deprecation. "We really must do something about it, Judge. I'd be the last one in the world to bother Miss Emily, but we've got to do something." That night the Board of Aldermen met—three graybeards and one younger man, a member of the rising generation.

"It's simple enough," he said. "Send her word to have her place cleaned up. Give her a certain time to do it in, and if she don't . . . "

"Dammit, sir," Judge Stevens said, "will you accuse a lady to her face of smelling bad?"

So the next night, after midnight, four men crossed Miss Emily's lawn and slunk about the house like burglars, sniffing along the base of the brickwork and at the cellar openings while one of them performed a regular sowing motion with his hand out of a sack slung from his shoulder. They broke open the cellar door and sprinkled lime there, and in all the outbuildings. As they recrossed the lawn, a window that had been dark was lighted and Miss Emily sat in it, the light behind her, and her upright torso motionless as that of an idol. They crept quietly across the lawn and into the shadow of the locusts that lined the street. After a week or two the smell went away.

That was when people had begun to feel really sorry for her. People in our town, remembering how old lady Wyatt, her great-aunt, had gone completely crazy at last, believed that the Griersons held themselves a little too high for what they really were. None of the young men were quite good enough for Miss Emily and such. We had long thought of them as a tableau, Miss Emily a slender figure in white in the background, her father a spraddled silhouette in the foreground, his back to her and clutching a horsewhip, the two of them framed by the back-flung front door. So when she got to be thirty and was still single, we were not pleased exactly, but vindicated; even with insanity in the family she wouldn't have turned down all of her chances if they had really materialized.

When her father died, it got about that the house was all that was left to her; and in a way, people were glad. At last they could pity Miss Emily. Being left alone, and a pauper, she had become humanized. Now she too would know the old thrill and the old despair of a penny more or less.

The day after his death all the ladies prepared to call at the house and offer condolence and aid, as is our custom. Miss Emily met them at the door, dressed as usual and with no trace of grief on her face. She told them that her father was not dead. She did that for three days, with the ministers calling on her, and the doctors, trying to persuade her to let them dispose of the body. Just as they were about to resort to law and force, she broke down, and they buried her father quickly.

We did not say she was crazy then. We believed she had to do that. We remembered all the young men her father had driven away, and we knew that with nothing left, she would have to cling to that which had robbed her, as people will.

III

She was sick for a long time. When we saw her again, her hair was cut short, making her look like a girl, with a vague resemblance to those angels in colored church windows—sort of tragic and serene.

The town had just let the contracts for paving the sidewalks, and in the summer after her father's death they began the work. The construction company came with niggers and mules and machinery, and a foreman named Homer Barron, a Yankee—a big, dark, ready man, with a big voice and eyes lighter than his face. The little boys would follow in groups to hear him cuss the niggers, and the niggers singing in time to the rise and fall of picks.

Pretty soon he knew everybody in town. Whenever you heard a lot of laughing anywhere about the square, Homer Barron would be in the center of the group. Presently we began to see him and Miss Emily on Sunday afternoons driving in the yellow-wheeled buggy and the matched team of bays from the livery stable.

At first we were glad that Miss Emily would have an interest, because the ladies all said, "Of course a Grierson would not think seriously of a Northerner, a day laborer." But there were still others, older people, who said that even grief could not cause a real lady to forget *noblesse oblige*—without calling it *noblesse oblige*. They just said, "Poor Emily. Her kinsfolk should come to her." She had some kin in Alabama; but years ago her father had fallen out with them over the estate of old lady Wyatt, the crazy woman, and there was no communication between the two families. They had not even been represented at the funeral.

And as soon as the old people said, "Poor Emily," the whispering began. "Do you suppose it's really so?" they said to one another. "Of course it is. What else could . . ." This behind their hands; rustling of craned silk and satin behind jalousies closed upon the sun of Sunday afternoon as the thin, swift clop-clop-clop of the matched team passed: "Poor Emily."

She carried her head high enough—even when we believed that she was fallen. It was as if she demanded more than ever the recognition of her dignity as the last Grierson; as if it had wanted that touch of earthiness to reaffirm her imperviousness. Like when she bought the rat poison, the arsenic. That was over a year after they had begun to say "Poor Emily," and while the two female cousins were visiting her.

"I want some poison," she said to the druggist. She was over thirty then, still a slight woman, though thinner than usual, with cold, haughty black eyes in a face the flesh of which was strained across the temples and about the eye-sockets as you imagine a lighthouse-keeper's face ought to look. "I want some poison," she said.

"Yes, Miss Emily. What kind? For rats and such? I'd recom—"

"I want the best you have. I don't care what kind."

The druggist named several. "They'll kill anything up to an elephant. But what you want is—"

"Arsenic," Miss Emily said. "Is that a good one?"

"Is . . . arsenic? Yes, ma'am. But what you want—"

"I want arsenic."

The druggist looked down at her. She looked back at him, erect, her face like a strained flag. "Why, of course," the druggist said. "If that's what you want. But the law requires you to tell what you are going to use it for."

Miss Emily just stared at him, her head tilted back in order to look him eye for eye, until he looked away and went and got the arsenic and wrapped it up. The Negro delivery boy brought her the package; the druggist didn't come back. When she opened the package at home there was written on the box, under the skull and bones: "For rats."

IV

So the next day we all said, "She will kill herself"; and we said it would be the best thing. When she had first begun to be seen with Homer Barron, we had said, "She will marry him." Then we said, "She will persuade him yet," because Homer himself had remarked—he liked men, and it was known that he drank with the younger men in the Elks' Club—that he was not a marrying man. Later we said, "Poor Emily" behind the jalousies as they passed on Sunday afternoon in the glittering buggy, Miss Emily with her head high and Homer Barron with his hat cocked and a cigar in his teeth, reins and whip in a yellow glove.

Then some of the ladies began to say that it was a disgrace to the town and a bad example to the young people. The men did not want to interfere, but at last the ladies forced the Baptist minister—Miss Emily's people were Episcopal—to call upon her. He would never divulge what happened during that interview, but he refused to go back again. The next Sunday they again drove about the streets, and the following day the minister's wife wrote to Miss Emily's relations in Alabama.

So she had blood-kin under her roof again and we sat back to watch developments. At first nothing happened. Then we were sure that they were to be married. We learned that Miss Emily had been to the jeweler's and ordered a man's toilet set in silver, with the letters H. B. on each piece. Two days later we learned that she had bought a complete outfit of men's clothing, including a nightshirt, and we said, "They are married." We were really glad. We were glad because the two female cousins were even more Grierson than Miss Emily had ever been.

So we were not surprised when Homer Barron—the streets had been finished some time since—was gone. We were a little disappointed that there was not a public blowing-off, but we believed that he had gone on to prepare for Miss Emily's coming, or to give her a chance to get rid of the cousins. (By that time it was a cabal, and we were all Miss Emily's allies to help circumvent the cousins.) Sure enough, after another week they departed. And, as we had expected all along, within three days Homer Barron was back in town. A neighbor saw the Negro man admit him at the kitchen door at dusk one evening.

And that was the last we saw of Homer Barron. And of Miss Emily for some time. The Negro man went in and out with the market basket, but the front door remained closed. Now and then we would see her at a window for a moment, as the men did that night when they sprinkled the lime, but for almost six months she did not appear on the streets. Then we knew that this was to be expected too; as if that quality of her father which had thwarted her woman's life so many times had been too virulent and too furious to die.

When we next saw Miss Emily, she had grown fat and her hair was turning gray. During the next few years it grew grayer and grayer until it attained an even pepper-and-salt iron-gray, when it ceased turning. Up to the day of her death at seventy-four it was still that vigorous iron-gray, like the hair of an active man.

From that time on her front door remained closed, save for a period of six or seven years, when she was about forty, during which she gave lessons in china-painting. She fitted up a studio in one of the downstairs rooms, where the daughters and granddaughters of Colonel Sartoris' contemporaries were sent to her with the same regularity and in the same spirit that they were sent to church on Sundays with a twenty-five-cent piece for the collection plate. Meanwhile her taxes had been remitted.

Then the newer generation became the backbone and the spirit of the town, and the painting pupils grew up and fell away and did not send their children to her with boxes of color and tedious brushes and pictures cut from the ladies' magazines. The front door closed upon the last one and remained closed for good. When the town got free postal delivery, Miss Emily alone refused to let them fasten the metal numbers above her door and attach a mailbox to it. She would not listen to them.

Daily, monthly, yearly we watched the Negro grow grayer and more stooped, going in and out with the market basket. Each December we sent her a tax notice, which would be returned by the post office a week later, unclaimed. Now and then we would see her in one of the downstairs windows—she had evidently shut up the top floor of the house—like the carven torso of an idol in a niche, looking or not looking at us, we could never tell which. Thus she passed from generation to generation—dear, inescapable, impervious, tranquil, and perverse.

And so she died. Fell ill in the house filled with dust and shadows, with only a doddering Negro man to wait on her. We did not even know she was sick; we had long since given up trying to get any information from the Negro. He talked to no one, probably not even to her, for his voice had grown harsh and rusty, as if from disuse.

She died in one of the downstairs rooms, in a heavy walnut bed with a curtain, her gray head propped on a pillow yellow and moldy with age and lack of sunlight.

V

The Negro met the first of the ladies at the front door and let them in, with their hushed, sibilant voices and their quick, curious glances, and then he disappeared. He walked right through the house and out the back and was not seen again.

The two female cousins came at once. They held the funeral on the second day, with the town coming to look at Miss Emily beneath a mass of bought flowers, with the crayon face of her father musing profoundly above the bier and the ladies sibilant and macabre; and the very old men—some in their brushed Confederate uniforms—on the porch and the lawn, talking of Miss Emily as if she had been a contemporary of theirs, believing that they had danced with her and courted her perhaps, confusing time with its mathematical progression, as the old do, to whom all the past is not a diminishing road but, instead, a huge meadow which no winter ever quite touches, divided from them now by the narrow bottle-neck of the most recent decade of years.

Already we knew that there was one room in that region above stairs which no one had seen in forty years, and which would have to be forced. They waited until Miss Emily was decently in the ground before they opened it.

The violence of breaking down the door seemed to fill this room with pervading dust. A thin, acrid pall as of the tomb seemed to lie everywhere upon this room decked and furnished as for a bridal: upon the valance curtains of faded rose color, upon the rose-shaded lights, upon the dressing table, upon the delicate array of crystal and the man's toilet things backed with tarnished silver, silver so tarnished that the monogram was obscured. Among them lay a collar and tie, as if they had just been removed, which, lifted, left upon the surface a pale crescent in the dust. Upon a chair hung the suit, carefully folded; beneath it the two mute shoes and the discarded socks.

The man himself lay in the bed.

For a long while we just stood there, looking down at the profound and fleshless grin. The body had apparently once lain in the attitude of an embrace, but now the long sleep that outlasts love, that conquers even the grimace of love, had cuckolded him. What was left of him, rotted beneath what was left of the nightshirt, had become inextricable from the bed in which he lay; and upon him and upon the pillow beside him lay that even coating of the patient and biding dust.

Then we noticed that in the second pillow was the indentation of a head. One of us lifted something from it, and leaning forward, that faint and invisible dust dry and acrid in the nostrils, we saw a long strand of iron-gray hair.

Matter Deleted from "A Rose for Emily"

The following passage appears in both the holograph manuscript and in the carbon typescript of the story, but is, for reasons not entirely clear, not part of the published story; it concludes part IV (*William Faulkner Manuscripts 9 These 13*. Ed. Noel Polk. New York: Garland, 1986. 210–12). This passage is unedited from Faulkner's original typescript. It was his practice not to use apostrophes in contractions of one syllable.

She died in one of the downstairs rooms, in a heavy walnut bed with a curtain, her gray head propped on a pillow yellow and moldy with age and lack of sunlight, her voice cold and strong to the last.

"But not till I'm gone," she said. "Dont you let a soul in until I'm gone, do you hear?" Standing beside the bed, his head in the dim light nimbused by a faint halo of napped, perfectly white hair, the negro made a brief gesture with his hand. Miss Emily lay with her eyes open, gazing into the opposite shadows of the room. Upon the coverlet her hands lay on her breast, gnarled, blue with age, motionless. "Hah," she said. "Then they can. Let 'em go up there and see what's in that room. Fools. Let 'em. Satisfy their minds that I am crazy. Do you think I am?" The negro made no reply, no movement. He stood above the bed, motionless, musing: a secret and unfathomable soul behind the death-mask of an ape and haloed like an angel. "Let 'em go up there and open that door. And you wont be the last one, either. Will you?"

"I wont have to," the negro said. "I know what's in that room. I dont have to see."

"Hah," Miss Emily said. "You do, do you. How long have you known?" Again he made that brief sign with his hand. Miss Emily had not turned her head. She stared into the shadows where the high ceiling was lost. "You should be glad. Now you can go to Chicago, like you've been talking about for thirty years. And with what you'll get for the house and furniture. . . . Colonel Sartoris has the will. He'll see they dont rob you."

"I dont want any house," the negro said.

"You cant help yourself. It's signed and sealed thirty-five years ago. Wasn't that our agreement when I found I couldn't pay you any wages? that you were to have everything that was left if you outlived me, and I was to bury you in a coffin with your name on a gold plate if I outlived you?" He said nothing. "Wasn't it?" Miss Emily said.

"I was young then. Wanted to be rich. But now I dont want any house."

"Not when you have wanted to go to Chicago for thirty years?" Their breathing was alike: each that harsh, rasping breath of the old, the short inhalations that do not reach the bottom of the lungs: tireless, precarious, on the verge of cessation for all time, as if anything might suffice: a word, a look. "What are you going to do, then?"

"Going to the poorhouse."

"The poorhouse? When I'm trying to fix you so you'll have neither to worry nor lift your hand as long as you live?"

"I dont want nothing," the negro said. "I'm going to the poorhouse. I already told them."

"Well," Miss Emily said. She had not moved her head, not moved at all. "Do you mind telling me why you want to go to the poorhouse?"

Again he mused. The room was still save for their breathing: it was as though they had both quitted all living and all dying; all the travail of mortality and of breath. "So I can set on that hill in the sun all day and watch them trains pass. See them at night too, with the engine puffing and lights in all the windows."

"Oh," Miss Emily said. Motionless, her knotted hands lying on the yellowed coverlet beneath her chin and her chin resting upon her breast, she appeared to muse intently, as though she were listening to dissolution setting up within her. "Hah," she said.

Then she died, and the negro met the first of the ladies. . . .

Discussion Questions

1. The narrator of the story calls the protagonist "Miss Emily," but the story's title very deliberately calls her "Emily." What are the implications of this distinction?

2. What is the effect on the story of the deletion of the several paragraphs at the end of part IV? How would the story be different, better or worse, if these paragraphs had been part of the story?

3. What is the function of Tobe? Does he add anything to the story that a white servant would not have or could not have?

4. Describe and characterize the narrator. Do you think the narrator is male or female? Black or white? What in the text would suggest one or the other? Does the narrator's race or gender matter? What is the narrator's relationship to the story he or she is telling?

5. In his novels, Faulkner was very interested in time and sequence. Why does he complicate the chronology of this story? What effect does the disrupted chronology have on our reading?

6. Do the three men in Emily Grierson's life—her father, her lover, and her servant—have anything in common?

7. Characterize "the town," the "community" of which the narrator speaks so often. Is the community of Jefferson in any way responsible for Emily's sad life?

8. Is gender an issue in this story? Consider the portrait the story paints of Emily's father. To what extent does he represent traditional masculine values?

9. Consider some of the class issues in the story. Why do the townspeople refer to Emily's family as "the high and mighty Griersons"? Why are they glad to see her poor, to "know the old thrill and the despair of a penny more or less"? How does the narrator contribute to class frictions?

10. Because Faulkner is so often identified as a "Southern" writer, "A Rose for Emily" is frequently seen as a story about quintessentially "Southern" values. What is peculiarly "Southern" about it? Could a story like this be set in another region? Why or why not?

Research Questions

1. Most of the scholarly commentators on "A Rose for Emily" say the story's jumbled chronology is a significant part of the telling. Compare and contrast each of the time lines offered by the scholars in this casebook with the evidence in the story itself. How important is the chronology to our understanding of the story? Is it possible, based on the story's evidence, to establish absolutely when all of these events take place? Is the jumbled chronology a result of carelessness on Faulkner's part, or is it a deliberate part of the story's structure and themes? If the latter, demonstrate how and why it is important.

2. In an interview with students at the University of Virginia, Faulkner said that "A Rose for Emily" is about a moral struggle, about "the conflict of conscience with glands, with the Old Adam. It was a conflict . . . between . . . God and Satan. . . . The conflict was in Miss Emily, that she knew that you do not murder people. She had been trained that you do not take a lover. You marry, you don't take a lover. She had broken all the laws of her tradition, her background, and she had finally broken the law of God too, which says you do not take human life. And she knew she was doing wrong, and that's why her own life was wrecked. Instead of murdering one lover, and then to go on and take another and when she used him up to murder him, she was expiating her crime." Discuss the story in terms of this moral conflict: if Emily knew she was doing wrong, why did she do it anyway?

3. Discuss the story's Freudian/Oedipal themes. Sullivan argues that Emily is to the narrator, "on the latent level . . . a mother to a child. This may sound absurd on first hearing, Miss Emily as a mother, the narrator as a child, for Miss Emily seems far from being a mother figure: she never married, had no children, lived alone, and took care of no one. . . . But I am not saying the narrator is her child, only that he is a child—and not chronologically but psychically: his psychic development is infantile. . . . She is a mother figure. For reasons not given in this story the narrator makes Miss Emily assume this role." Compare her reading of the Oedipal content of the story with that of other commentators.

4. Discuss the story's narrator and the general problem of narration in the story. Ruth Sullivan's essay, for example, argues for a narrator who is vitally implicated in Emily's life, whereas Isaac Rodman proposes a narrator distinguished by his cool, ironic, and poetic distance from her. This narrator stands somewhere between a traditional third-person

omniscient narrator, one who knows all, and a first-person narrator who is directly involved in the events he or she is narrating and whose knowledge and understanding of the events being narrated is limited. Does the story itself make it possible for us to decide between Sullivan and Rodman, or must we defer to Robert Crosman's sense of the story's deliberate refusal to explain everything?

5. Rodman calls the townspeople's "seeming inability . . . to associate the smell of decaying meat with the disappearance of Homer Barron" a "willful blindness." Discuss the community as the narrator creates it for us. What is the community's stake in Emily's life and (mis)fortune? What is its cumulative effect on the way Emily lives her life?

Secondary Sources

Each of the ten sources in this section* offers insights into "A Rose for Emily"—insights that can help you understand, enjoy, and perhaps write about the story. The sources included in this section range from an interview with William Faulkner to critical articles commenting on specific ideas. You may use these sources to generate ideas that could be developed into a paper, or you may find materials to support a topic you have already chosen. After you have read these sources, you can use the bibliography at the back of this book to locate further resources pertaining to Faulkner's life and works. Remember to document any words or ideas that you borrow from these and any other sources.

FREDERICK L. GWYNN AND JOSEPH BLOTNER

Faulkner in the University: Class Conferences at the University of Virginia, 1957–1958

Editor's note: During the spring semesters of 1957 and 1958, Faulkner was writer in residence at the University of Virginia. Among his duties was to meet with students who wanted to discuss his work with him. These class interviews were recorded and published in *Faulkner in the University: Class Conferences at the University of Virginia 1957–1958*. The following passages record his responses to questions about "A Rose for Emily."

Q. Was the "Rose for Emily" an idea or a character? Just how did you go about it?

---

* Note that several of these articles do not use the documentation style recommended by the Modern Language Association and explained in the Appendix.

A. That came from a picture of the strand of hair on the pillow. It was a ghost story. Simply a picture of a strand of hair on the pillow in the abandoned house. [26]

. . .

Q. Sir, in "A Rose for Emily" is it possible to take Homer Barron and Emily and sort of show that one represents the South and the North? Is there anything on your part there trying to show the North and the South in sort of a battle, maybe Miss Emily representing the South coming out victorious in the rather odd way that she did?

A. That would be only incidental. I think that the writer is too busy trying to create flesh-and-blood people that will stand up and cast a shadow to have time to be conscious of all the symbolism that he may put into what he does or what people may read into it. That if he had time to—that is, if one individual could write the authentic, credible, flesh-and-blood character and at the same time deliver the message, maybe he would, but I don't believe any writer is capable of doing both, that he's got to choose one of the two: either he is delivering a message or he's trying to create flesh-and-blood, living, suffering, anguishing human beings. And as any man works out of his past, since any man—no man is himself, he's the sum of his past, and in a way, if you can accept the term, of his future too. And this struggle between the South and the North could have been a part of my background, my experience, without me knowing it. [47–48]

. . .

Q. Sir, it has been argued that "A Rose for Emily" is a criticism of the North, and others have argued saying that it is a criticism of the South. Now, could this story, shall we say, be more properly classified as a criticism of the times?

A. Now that I don't know, because I was simply trying to write about people. The writer uses environment—what he knows—and if there's a symbolism in which the lover represented the North and the woman who murdered him represents the South, I don't say that's not valid and not there, but it was no intention of the writer to say, Now let's see, I'm going to write a piece in which I will use a symbolism for the North and another symbol for the South, that he was simply writing about people, a story which he thought was tragic and true, because it came out of the human heart, the human aspiration, the human—the conflict of conscience with glands, with the Old Adam. It was a conflict not between the North and the South so much as between, well you might say, God and Satan.

Q. Sir, just a little more on that thing. You say it's a conflict between God and Satan. Well, I don't quite understand what you mean. Who is—did one represent the—

A. The conflict was in Miss Emily, that she knew that you do not murder people. She had been trained that you do not take a lover. You marry, you don't take a lover. She had broken all the laws of her tradition, her background, and she had finally broken the law of God too, which says you do not take human life. And she knew she was doing wrong, and that's why her own life was wrecked. Instead of murdering one lover, and then to go on and take another and when she used him up to murder him, she was expiating her crime.

Q. . . . She did do all the things that she had been taught not to do, and being a sensitive sort of a woman, it was sure to have told on her, but do you think it's fair to feel pity for her, because in a way she made her adjustment, and it seems to have wound up in a happy sort of a way— certainly tragic, but maybe it suited her just fine.

A. Yes, it may have, but then I don't think that one should withhold pity simply because the subject of the pity, object of pity, is pleased and satisfied. I think the pity is in the human striving against its own nature, against its own conscience. That's what deserves the pity. It's not the state of the individual, it's man in conflict with his heart, or with his fellows, or with his environment—that's what deserves the pity. It's not that the man suffered, or that he fell off the house, or was run over by the train. It's that he was—that man is trying to do the best he can with his desires and impulses against his own moral conscience, and the conscience of, the social conscience of his time and his place—the little town he must live in, the family he's a part of. [58–59]

. . .

Q. What is the meaning of the title "A Rose for Emily"?

A. Oh, it's simply the poor woman had had no life at all. Her father had kept her more or less locked up and then she had a lover who was about to quit her, she had to murder him. It was just "A Rose for Emily"—that's all. [87–88]

. . .

Q. I was wondering, one of your short stories, "A Rose for Emily," what ever inspired you to write this story . . . ?

A. That to me was another sad and tragic manifestation of man's condition in which he dreams and hopes, in which he is in conflict with himself or with his environment or with others. In this case there was the young girl with a young girl's normal aspirations to find love and then a husband and a family, who was brow-beaten and kept down by her father, a selfish man who didn't want her to leave home because he wanted a housekeeper, and it was a natural instinct of—repressed which—you can't repress it—you can mash it down but it comes up somewhere else and very likely in a tragic form, and that was simply another manifestation of man's injustice to man, of the poor tragic human being struggling with its own heart, with others, with its environment, for the simple things which all human beings want. In that case it was a young girl that just wanted to be loved and to love and to have a husband and a family.

Q. And that purely came from your imagination?

A. Well, the story did but the condition is there. It exists. I didn't invent that condition, I didn't invent the fact that young girls dream of someone to love and children and a home, but the story of what her own particular tragedy was was invented, yes. . . . [184–85]

. . .

Q. Is "A Rose for Emily" all fiction?

A. Yes sir. Yes sir, that's all fiction, for the reason I said, too. If any time a writer writes anything that seems at all familiar to anybody anywhere, he gets a letter about it, and if they think he's got enough money, he's sued, too, so he's awful careful not to write anything he ever saw himself, or anybody ever told him. [199]

TERRY HELLER

The Telltale Hair: A Critical Study of William Faulkner's "A Rose for Emily"

The Soul selects her own Society—
Then—shuts the Door—
To her divine Majority—
Present no more—
Unmoved—she notes the Chariots—pausing
At her low Gate—
Unmoved—an Emperor be kneeling
Upon her Mat—
I've known her—from an ample nation—

Choose One—
Then—close the valves of her attention—
Like Stone—
EMILY DICKINSON

During the more than four decades since the first publication of William Faulkner's story "A Rose for Emily," two general questions seem to have attracted significant critical attention. The more recently flourishing discussion of the narration has centered on the narrative voice, whether it is distinct from or coincident with the voice or voices of the town. Those readers who have made strong arguments for a distinct persona have differed widely in characterizing it. Nicklaus Happel, for example, believes that the narrator is somewhat aloof from the town and that, in the course of his narrative, he shows sympathy for Emily to atone for past neglect.[1] Ruth Sullivan, in a long article devoted exclusively to the narration, asserts that psychoanalysis of the narrator shows him to be not only the most important character, but also the villain of the story.[2] The larger portion of critical discussion has centered on the nature and cause of the aberration which leads Emily to kill Homer and keep his body in her bedroom. On this question, also, there is little agreement. Is Emily a black widow who devours her unsuspecting lover? A desperate and slightly crazed spinster who kills to possess him? Denied natural outlets for her emotions, perhaps she is forced into madness or a fantasy world? Is she a victim, then, of time, the town, her father, or her own repressed sexuality?[3] Some of these interpretations suggest that we should sympathize with Emily and some do not. Others suggest that our feelings should be mixed.

Such varied disagreement about our basic responses to the story may indicate that it, like "The Turn of the Screw," simply does not seem to allow us to reach a single definitive understanding. On the other hand, it may be that we have been asking the wrong questions or asking our questions in the wrong way. Let us then attempt to look at "A Rose for Emily" from a slightly different point of view, keeping in mind the major questions that have puzzled other critics, but also trying to find new or, at least, untried questions that might help to increase our understanding and appreciation.

Beginning with section one, let us look closely at the text and our responses to it. The first sentence introduces the antagonists:

> When Miss Emily Grierson died, our whole town went to her funeral:
> the men through a sort of respectful affection for a fallen monument, the

women mostly out of curiosity to see the inside of her house, which no one save an old man-servant—a combined gardener and cook—had seen in at least ten years.[4]

Emily's clause is subordinate; the town is the subject of the sentence. Such a construction used by an artist who compared the short story to the lyric poem in its demands for exactness and economy, should lead us to suspect that the town may require as much of our attention as Emily.[5] Besides telling us that Emily is a spinster who has not been visited in ten years, this sentence also provides important clues to the town's attitudes toward Emily. The town comes to her funeral, not in grief to mourn the passing of a beloved member of the community, but out of curiosity and respect for a defunct institution. In the first sentence, we are already disposed to side with Emily as a victim for there is no evidence that she is regarded with deserved hate or disgust. On the contrary, she seems to have been a pillar of the community.

Although the second paragraph seems to move our attention from Emily and the town to her house—a house such as we often see in Gothic Romances—we are shown a similar set of antagonists. The house appears to be the victim of the town too. Having been surrounded by commercial interests, it is "stubborn and coquettish" in its decay. The last sentence of the paragraph suggests that Emily's removal to the cemetery is parallel to the house's removal from selectness. The house stands in a neighborhood of obliterated august names as her grave is among "the ranked and anonymous" graves of Civil War soldiers. The parallel works in reverse also, suggesting that the house is a kind of tomb. In each case, Emily and her house are not the agents but the victims. Of what are they the victims? The house seems clearly to be decaying, a victim of time, yet it may not necessarily be a natural process that changes the most select street to a commercial area. As Emily's house is invaded by the townspeople in the first paragraph, so her neighborhood is invaded by commercial interests rather than preserved for the value it may once have had. It is suggested, then, that the men's "respectful affection" is a hollow emotion, hollow as would be the suggestion that her house is still standing because of the town's sentimental nostalgia.

There is also in this second paragraph a curious statement, the judgment that the house is "an eyesore among eyesores." This phrase is unique in the first two paragraphs because it is the only purely evaluative statement we find. It is significant because it alerts us that we are perceiving through a consciousness that not only sees and generalizes, but also judges. Before we have seen an actual incident, we have a sense of antagonistic forces and a judging narrative consciousness.

The remainder of the first section presents a brief history of Emily's taxes, beginning with their remission by Colonel Sartoris: ". . . Colonel Sartoris, the mayor—he who fathered the edict that no Negro woman should appear on the streets without an apron—remitted her taxes . . ." The syntax encourages us to see the mayor's two acts as similar. Emily, as impoverished aristocracy, is somewhat like the former slaves; she becomes a duty, obligation, and care. The Colonel's apparently charitable action is qualified by his motives, which appear to be based more on the maintenance of a rigid class order than on respectful affection. The mayor treats her not as an individual human being in need, but as a class, as a Lady Aristocrat. The newer generation recognizes no such category and decides she must pay her taxes. The new aldermen dehumanize Emily into a Faceless Citizen. From them she receives an impersonal tax notice, a formal letter, an offer from the mayor to meet at the place of her choosing, and finally, a deputation. In the second pair of paragraphs we see two generations in relation to Emily. The generations are similar in that they both choose to deal with an idea of Emily, rather than with Emily herself; they are different in that they have different ideas of her and, therefore, approach her and her taxes differently.

Another pair of paragraphs precedes the first dramatic incident. In them we see the interior of the house that the ladies were so curious about and we see Emily. The atmosphere of the house reminds us again of Gothic Romance. It is tomblike, dusty, dark, and damp, with a stairway that mounts into shadow. The room we see is dominated by a crayon portrait of Emily's long dead father on a tarnished gilt easel. When Emily appears, we begin to see that she resembles her house. A gold chain disappears into her belt just as the stair disappears into shadow, and her cane has a tarnished gold head. Her appearance is striking,

> Her skeleton was small and spare; perhaps that was why what would have
> been merely plumpness in another was obesity in her. She looked bloated like
> a body long submerged in motionless water, and of that pallid hue.

This passage begins with a kind of apology for her heaviness that teases the imagination. First she is small and spare, then pleasingly plump, but by the end of the first sentence she is obese. Three words later she is bloated and by the end of the passage she has been transformed from a little old lady into a bloated corpse as decayed as the house. How do we respond to such a description? If, through the hints that we may be in Gothic Romance, we have come to expect a Gothic heroine, we may be surprised when we learn she is small and fat. If in spite of our developing sympathy, the description tempts us to see her as a Gothic villainess, the apologetic narrative approach to her appearance prevents us from succumbing. But how are we affected when she balloons into a drowned corpse? Looking like a corpse, she may be sinister, yet on the other hand, she may deserve sympathy—especially if her appearance is the result of the same kind of process that has made the house into an eyesore. The narrator by introducing us so gently to her ghastly appearance seems to have shown some sympathy for her, reinforcing the sympathy we already feel for what appears to be the helpless victim of powerful and careless forces.

Before we see her act, before we have any knowledge of her character, we are disposed to see Emily as victimized. The town shows little sympathy for her. Two generations have viewed her as a stereotype rather than as a living person. As Americans we usually side with the underdog, yet we are not sure how to judge Emily. She seems both pathetic and sinister. The interior of her house is both sad and frightening. One of the frightening things about her and her house is exemplified by the staircase and the gold chain both of which produce lines that frustrate the eye, causes without effects. We are led to believe there is a watch at the end of the chain because the deputation hears the ticking, but the ticking is an effect without a visible cause and adds to our sense of uneasiness by suggesting mystery and disorder. We should now be alerted to watch for a continuation of this pattern.

When we finally see her act, our responses are both clarified and clouded. As Americans, we tend to support Emily against an invasion of tax collectors, yet she seems not to need support. In the confrontation, we see her standing framed in a doorway, dominating the room as her father's portrait dominated before she entered. She is dignified and powerful as she vanquishes them. Her triumph is undercut, however, by the narrator's parenthetical remark that her authority, Colonel Sartoris, has been dead for ten years. That she acts as if the mayor is still alive is another unexplained action like an effect without a cause. Is it possible she does not know he is dead? Does she live in a fantasy world where the people she likes never die or is she perversely pretending ignorance? By defeating the deputation she upsets our expectations that she will be victimized and earns our admiration for her strength. At the same time, she confronts us with disturbing mysteries about her character and motives.

A series of confrontations between Emily and Jefferson takes place in the following sections. When the aldermen attempt to take care of the smell without confronting her, she catches and shames them. The next confrontation concerns her refusal to admit her father's death. On the surface, the town defeats her, bending her to its will. Emily profoundly shocks the town, however, and "she broke down" after a three-day struggle followed by a long illness and a kind of resurrection. In part three, she refuses, or perhaps fails, to play the part of Fallen Woman when the town thinks she is fallen. She also succeeds in buying arsenic without satisfying the law's requirement. Her victories continue into part four when she vanquishes the Baptist minister and when the town's female-relations strategy backfires. Then, apparently, she suffers complete defeat. Homer disappears and the town is morally triumphant. The suspected affair is at an end and Emily has not married a Yankee day laborer. Throughout the rest of part four, Emily leads the isolated spinster's life, doing the things spinsters may be expected to do: teaching china painting, refusing a mailbox and house number, and finally dying alone in her decaying house. In part five the town is completely in control. They bury her and behave as they wish at her funeral. The old men change her past to suit their befuddled fantasies. It is as if all are eager to remove the old monument and to replace her house with a cotton gin or a filling station. Then her bridal chamber reveals that once again she has vanquished the town and that even after her death, Jefferson has failed finally to understand and deal with her.

As we witness these confrontations, we seem to learn much about the town but relatively little about Emily. Through what the town feels, says, thinks, and does we gradually obtain a fairly clear idea of its character as a group. For example, there is a cluster of events which do not surprise the town. The ladies are not surprised when the smell develops because a man could not take care of a kitchen and because, "It was another link between the gross, teeming world and the high and mighty Griersons." Believing Emily and Homer are married, the town is not surprised when Homer is gone or when he returns after the cousins leave. Emily's isolation after the disappearance of Homer is to be expected as her reassertion of morality.

There are things about which the town is sad and glad. The townspeople begin to be really sorry for her after the smell goes away because they remember how her great aunt went "completely crazy" and how her father kept suitors away. On the other hand, they are "not pleased exactly, but vindicated" when she is still single at thirty. They are glad when her father dies and leaves her a pauper because, at last, they can pity her and believe her equal to themselves for "Now she too would know the old thrill and the old despair of a penny more or less." They are glad when Emily and Homer are seen together, but begin to say "poor Emily" when the old people gossip enough to convince them she is a Fallen Woman. They are convinced it would be the best thing if she killed herself with the poison she buys. They are *really* glad when they think Emily and Homer are married because they want to be rid of her female cousins, but are sorry when there is no public party. The town in being glad, sad, and not surprised reveals itself to be not only unsympathetic, but unmistakably vicious.

As distinguished from what the town feels, the things that the town says, believes, and does not only reveal viciousness and callousness, but seem to reflect limited inductive powers. For example, the town believes Homer will marry Emily, but he deserts her. They believe she is fallen, but she does not behave as a Fallen Woman. They believe she will kill herself with the poison and she does not. They summon the cousins to prevent Emily from behaving immorally, then are willing to countenance the affair and the marriage in order to be rid of those cousins. They say she will marry Homer, then discover that he likes men and is not a marrying man. They say she will eventually persuade him, but we never know if she does. In general they are wrong—as it is almost certain that they are wrong about the cause of the smell and the fact of the marriage. The town's actions reveal callousness, viciousness, hypocrisy, meddling, and a general inability to understand the meanings of events. The people of Jefferson prove themselves completely unable to sympathize with and understand Emily. Every man who attempts to coerce Emily, except perhaps Homer and her father, leaves her house never to return in her lifetime. Even the druggist does not return from his supply room after confronting her.

Why does the town fail so completely? Its major failing seems to be either one of vision, which in turn results in one of sympathy, or vice versa. In order to account for and deal with Emily, the people constantly resort to categorization. We have seen that Colonel Sartoris remits her taxes in order to preserve a kind of status quo, that he assigns static identities to people and classes, identities which then define appropriate responses. Because she is a poor Lady she should not have to pay taxes; because she is a Lady, Judge Stevens cannot tell her to her face that she smells bad and the aldermen are forced into their ludicrous escapade; and because she is a Lady, the plebeian townspeople envy her and are glad to discover evidence that she may be ordinary. They, especially the older generation, are eager to turn her status against her when she is courted by a Yankee day laborer. The new generation has the same limitation in a different form. For them Emily is a Faceless Citizen who must be made to pay her taxes and forced to "clean up her place," who must comply with the law in regard to dead fathers and buying poison, and who should have a mailbox on her house. Whereas the older generation felt that sending their children to Emily to learn china painting was a duty or obligation like sending them to Sunday School, the new generation does not even feel the obligation. In effect, the new generation's approach is little different from the old, yet we prefer the latter because its roots in human feeling and concern are still discernible.

The Lady Aristocrat and the Faceless Citizen are not the only categories applied to Emily, though most of the others can be seen as extensions of the former. When the town sees her as the heroine-in-white of a melodramatic tableau in which her father threatens off suitors with his horsewhip, she is expected to do the kinds of things a melodramatic heroine usually does: to cling to her dead father despite his supposed cruelty, to kill herself with poison when her honor is sullied, and to isolate herself in her house when her lover deserts her or when she has ordered him to leave. When she is a Fallen Woman, she is a bad influence on children and ought not to ride with her beau on Sunday afternoon or to hold her head high. She is then to be gossiped about behind jalousied windows, preached to by middle-class ministers, and protected by female relations. Although she apparently sees qualities in Homer that make him worthy of her attention, the town dismisses him using the categories of Northerner and Day Laborer. In parts one, two, and four, Emily is almost always described as framed in a door, window, or picture so that we come to see her as confined in the vision of the town. For us, however, the frames seem to make her into a kind of portrait of an unknown and mysterious woman the special object of our sympathy and wonder as she is the object of the town's lack of sympathy.

Though it is not really clear whether stereotyping is a cause or an effect of lack of sympathy, it seems rather clear that the problem with the categories is that they falsify their object, making sympathy difficult. Categorizing Emily as Lady Aristocrat, the confederate veterans at the funeral even falsify the public record, remembering things that could never have been. Because the town unfailingly bases its approach to Emily on stereotypical expectations, it never sees her as the very human person we believe her to be. The older generation fails because it is decadent and its categories have become inflexible; the new because it is impersonal; the town as a whole because Emily's class identity provokes pettiness and jealousy in them and because they tend to see her in terms of stock melodramatic stereotypes. All fail to see the human Emily. Their vision is so limited by these categories which, instead of being shortcuts, are barriers to sympathy, that they are always ludicrous in their attempts to understand and deal with her. She never does quite what they expect. Regardless of which comes first, the failure of vision and the lack of sympathy are mutually supporting. They form a closed system of which Emily appears, in spite of her resistance, to be a nearly helpless victim.

We find, then, that the town's actions, feelings, and motives are scrutinized rather closely. The quality of their actions disposes us to sympathize with Emily as a victim of careless cruelty. We noted in our discussion of the first section that we felt pressure to sympathize with Emily as a victim of the town at her funeral and concerning her taxes, but we also felt ambiguously about her character upon first seeing her. Let us attempt to determine how we should feel about Emily through an examination of some of the means that are used for controlling our responses. We can begin by looking at the narration.

As stated previously, the narration of "A Rose for Emily" has been the subject of varied controversy. A particularly thorny problem in trying to understand the narration is the alteration of the chronology. The story seems to be told by a participant in at least some of the events described, yet all of the events are complete at the time of the telling. Emily's funeral is over before the story begins and the last scene of the story is in the past tense. Therefore, the narrator must suspect now, as he apparently did not at the time, the causal relation of the poison, the disappearance of Homer, and the smell, yet he gives us the smell in part two, the poison in part three, and the disappearance in four. One apparent effect of this alteration is to prevent us from easily perceiving the possible relation of these seemingly isolated events. Another effect might be to emphasize both the speaker's distance from the events—as he is able to re-order them—and the town's lack of sympathetic understanding which he presumably shared when the events took place. At at least one point, the narrator fails to give us pertinent information we assume that he has: he must know in what order Emily bought the toilet articles, the clothing, and the poison. In both the alteration of chronology and this withholding of available information, the narrator seems to be purposive. In the second case, he increases our difficulty in understanding Emily's intentions. Does she intend to seduce Homer into marriage or death, or the latter only if the former fails?

In the first section of the story, we noted a separation of cause and effect in the matters of the stairway, the chain, the ticking, and Emily's belief that Colonel Sartoris is alive. The silent minister, the purchase of the poison, the smell, the return of Homer, the body on the bed, and a host of other phenomena seem also to fall into one of these two classes: floating effects or dangling causes. Now we can see, however, that this separation may be a deliberate narrative strategy, that it serves several purposes and is essential to our reading experience. The separation of cause and effect obscures the obvious pattern of events for us very much as does the alteration of the chronology, thereby keeping our judgments about Emily in suspension and allowing the narrator to build sympathy for her before we can suspect what she may have done. It also reveals another facet of the town's failure to sympathize with her. The town's categories encourage the isolation of causes and effects, increasing the probability of interpretive error. Furthermore, a series of mysteries is created which we strongly suspect to have different explanations from those offered by the town. As we learn to distrust the town, we begin to wonder what is really happening between Emily and Homer. Is there really an affair? Does she marry him? These mysteries increase in number and depth as the story continues.

The patterns we have seen in the narration thus far seem to indicate that the story is told by a single voice. We have also seen evidence of narrative sympathy for Emily in the first part of the story. Is there other evidence of narrative sympathy? The first sentence of part two, "So she vanquished them, horse and foot, just as she had vanquished their fathers thirty years before about the smell" clearly indicates admiration for Emily. The last two paragraphs of part four show great narrative sympathy for Emily. The sentence which precedes them, "Thus she passed from generation to generation—dear, inescapable, impervious, tranquil, and perverse" applies five adjectives to Emily, only four of which we have seen portrayed. To whom is Emily dear, unless in the sense of being costly? Perhaps at this point she has become dear in another sense to the narrator and to us. The last two paragraphs of the section tell of Emily's dying alone in pitiable circumstances without anyone even knowing she is ill. The narrative tone is one of pity for the forlorn and neglected Emily. In part five the narrator seems to separate himself from the people and to judge them as he tells us that the flowers were bought by relatives rather than cut by the townspeople, that the ladies are curious and macabre, and that the old veterans distorted her past in their memories. Even though the townspeople seem, for once, to do the decent thing by not opening the room until she is buried, they have pried enough to know that the door will have to be forced. The consistent narrative sympathy for Emily is not only in contrast to the town's attitude, but presumably, also in contrast to the narrator's own attitude at the time the events took place.

How, then, does this narrative attitude affect us as readers? The teller's sympathy reinforces our similar emotions. Yet, even though we tend to take Emily's part against all tax collectors, mailmen, and busybodies, we are not required to sympathize with and admire her without qualification. The narrator appears also to be rather uncertain about Emily's true character. We have already noted our ambiguous response to her initial appearance. Emily does many other things that make us uneasy about her: thinking Colonel Sartoris is alive ten years after his death, keeping her father's body, buying poison, and having a smell about her house. Subtle and macabre suggestions of perverse madness, i.e., incest, cannibalism, and necrophilia, appear in the first four parts and receive some support in the fifth. Balancing these disturbing elements is another set of facts and appearances. She appears to really love Homer if the expensive gifts she buys him are any indication, and perhaps her father, if we can judge by the ever present portrait which she herself may have done. She appears to treat both men as if they were not dead after they die. Such treatment may indicate either madness or love. When the lime spreaders open her cellar, they reveal that there is no secret there as is often the case in Gothic houses. When she has her hair cut, she looks like an angel. Ten years after Homer's disappearance, she offers china painting lessons to the village children, reminding us of kindhearted Hepzibah Pyncheon and her little shop. Even the final scene in the dusty bridal chamber may be as pathetic as it is gruesome.

These apparently conflicting cues are arranged so that as our suspicion of the truth about Emily grows, one set confirms and the other allays those suspicions. When Homer disappears into the house one evening, we are almost certain that we know the truth even if the town does not. Almost immediately, however, we see Emily become a fat and lonely spinster. We are asked to pity poor Emily who teaches children to paint and dies alone on a moldy bed. Our suspended judgment is never allowed to settle itself. We pity and admire Emily without being certain that she needs or deserves such sympathy. The story is so constructed that we sympathize with Emily without understanding her, whereas the town, thinking it understands her, is shown to lack sympathy. At the same time we share, to a degree, a sense of the town's error as we are tempted to see Emily in terms of certain literary conventions, i.e., Gothic Romance or Melodrama, from which she continually diverges.

The last scene of "A Rose for Emily" has the form of a revelation. The secret room is entered and light falls on the dark mystery of Emily's life. How does this scene affect our feelings and knowledge about Emily? Conventionally, we may expect resolution of conflicting emotions and the explanation of mysteries. First let us examine our emotional response to the scene. Just before it, our pity for Emily and contempt for the town have reached their highest points. Then we are led into the dusty room and shown everything in it, the details of a rose-colored tomblike bridal chamber. The scene is first pathetic, expressive of the fulfillment Emily never had, the mausoleum of a girl's hopes covered with dust. Then the narrator points out the body that once lay in an attitude of embrace and describes it as victim of the same forces that outlast love, time, and death. Grisly as it is, the scene is one of frustrated tenderness. If we are horrified at what Emily appears to have done, we are at the same time asked to pity the woman for whom this scene represents nearly all the love and companionship she has known for forty years and to admire the woman who has once again thwarted the town's attempts to categorize her. It seems to me that each of the emotions that Emily arouses in us—pity, admiration, and horror—is here felt to its extreme. Does the long, gray hair finally horrify or does it move the reader to tears and awe? The final scene stubbornly refuses to resolve the conflicting responses that have been cultivated in the reader throughout the story.

What mysteries does the last scene solve? It strengthens our suspicions about the causal relation of the poison, Homer's disappearance, and the smell, but does not confirm those suspicions. In fact, the narrator teasingly encourages the reader to doubt the relation. The monogram on the silver is obscured. The body is not identified, nor is it in an attitude to indicate a violent death from arsenic. It is possible that Homer and Emily lived together in the house, secretly of course, for several years. Such a suggestion seems absurd, but the very fact that it can be defended illustrates how little we really learn in the climactic scene. Mysteries about Emily's actions remain unsolved: if she had an affair with Homer, if she killed him, and if she used the poison. New mysteries are created: if she lay with the corpse and if so, for how long. These are only a few of the mysterious events that remain mysterious and the greatest mystery, too, remains as dark as ever. If she did all the things it appears she did, why? As was stated in the introduction to this essay, this question has absorbed much critical effort since the story's publication, yet if my analysis is correct, that was probably not the most fruitful question to attempt to answer because neither the narrator, the town, nor the reader has enough information to answer it. Instead of trying to explain Emily, the narrator does his best to present all the difficulties in the way of such an explanation. The narrator shows us a group of incidents in which the town uses stereotypes that always fail to account for her. Finally, the narrator has more information than we because he knows the order in which the gifts and the poison were bought. With that knowledge, we might possibly guess with more certainty if she planned to murder Homer and decorate the room or if the gifts mean that she loved him. Knowing less than the narrator and no more than the town, how do we dare to guess at Emily's motives given the examples of his restraint and the town's failure? So Emily remains very much a mystery. We never see her thinking and must infer her motives from a small group of external actions. As so many critics have so ably shown, even after agreement is reached on the content and extent of her actions, those actions admit of numerous explanations.

We have seen that the story focuses on the relationship between Emily and Jefferson; specifically on the ways in which the town interprets and acts on the information it gathers about her. The narrator recounts a series of incidents in which the town attempts and fails to deal with Emily. In each case, the failure seems to result in some way from a previous failure to sympathize with and understand Emily. She, on the other hand, is seen only through a few brief actions and her motives are not represented except as they are guessed by the town. We have also seen that we are made to sympathize with Emily despite our ignorance of her and the conflicting cues we receive about her moral nature. We are encouraged to feel about Emily in a way that the town fails to feel so that we come to appreciate her human uniqueness as the town does not. Furthermore, we have seen that the narrator, though a participant in some of the events described, is now critical of the town and sympathetic toward Emily. "A Rose for Emily," then, shows us not only the barriers to understanding and sympathy which lead inevitably to violence and suffering, but also the means of overcoming those barriers through compassionate human sympathy, i.e., making the effort to understand another through imaginative identification rather than in terms of rigid codes of conduct and categories of perception. The story is not easily optimistic however, for it is only after her death, when the hair is found on the indented pillow and all the damage has been irrevocably done, that anyone begins to understand how the town has apparently victimized Emily and how grandly she seems to have resisted victimization. In *Absalom, Absalom!* Quentin and Shreve, through imaginative identification with Henry and Charles, come to learn "what must be truth" about the murder of Charles, but in this story no one ever learns the whole truth about Emily. Yet we sympathize with her, for in the end her acts are no more bizarre than the town's, while in many ways she seems immeasurably more valuable and grand than all of Jefferson. The town attempts throughout her life to treat her as we see it treating her in the first two paragraphs of the story, as if she were dead. If she makes Homer into a corpse, who makes her into one? We see no anguish or pain in the town, but we see evidence enough to imagine what Emily may have suffered. At least one person, forced into the realm of light by that dusty room, seems to have realized the possibility of her suffering and to have been brought by that realization to the point of saying as Faulkner said,

> . . . I don't think that one should withhold pity simply because the . . . object of pity, is pleased and satisfied. I think the pity is in the human striving against its own nature, against its own conscience . . . it's man in conflict with his heart, or with his fellows, or with his environment—that's what deserves the pity.[6]

NOTES

[1] N. Happel, "William Faulkner's 'A Rose for Emily,'" *Die Neueren Sprachen*, 9 (1962), 396–404. Reprinted in M. Thomas Inge, ed. *William Faulkner: A Rose for Emily* (Columbus: Charles E. Merrill Pub. Co., 1970), as translated by Alfred Kolb.

[2] R. Sullivan, "The Narrator in 'A Rose for Emily,'" *The Journal of Narrative Technique*, 1 (September 1971), 159–78. K. P. Kempton in *The Short Story* (Cambridge: Harvard University Press, 1954), pp. 104–06, suggests that there is a town-narrator who appears to become more visible as the story progresses. F. C. Watkins in "The Structure of 'A Rose for Emily,'" *Modern Language Notes*, 69 (November 1954), 508–10, seems to see the townspeople as a kind of group narrator. Brooks and Warren in *Understanding Fiction* (2nd Ed. New York: Appleton Century Crofts, 1959), pp. 350–54, suggests that the town-narrator may be an important character in his own right. All of the above except Ruth Sullivan's article are reprinted in M. Thomas Inge, ed. *William Faulkner: A Rose for Emily* (Columbus: Charles E. Merrill Pub. Co., 1970).

[3] Brooks and Warren believe that Emily heroically resists restrictive local values. C. W. M. Johnson, "Faulkner's 'A Rose for Emily,'" *Explicator*, 6 (May 1948), item 45, argues that, far from heroic, she resists change as the South has done and that her just punishment is to live with death. R. B. West in "Faulkner's 'A Rose for Emily,'" *Explicator*, 7 (October 1948), item 8, and in "Atmosphere and Theme in Faulkner's 'A Rose for Emily,'" from *The Writer in the Room* (East Lansing: Michigan State University Press, 1949), pp. 205–11, defending Emily, states that she resists time because she has been betrayed by it in the forms of her father who represents the Old Order and Homer who represents the New Order. In her attempts to overcome time, she is at once monstrous, heroic, and tragic. C. A. Allen, "William Faulkner: Comedy and the Purpose of Humor," *Arizona Quarterly*, 16 (Spring 1960), 60, thinks that Emily takes Homer in defiance as a father-substitute, then kills him to insure possession when he threatens to leave her. Dominating her world, she is unable to distinguish between reality and illusion. W. V. O'Connor, *The Tangled Fire of William Faulkner* (Minneapolis: University of Minnesota Press, 1954), p. 68, agrees that Emily retreats into a fantasy world, but because she has been denied natural outlets for her emotions. Irving Howe in *William Faulkner* (2nd Ed. New York: Vintage, 1962), p. 265, sees the story as one of the decay of human sensibility from "false gentility to genteel perversion." Irving Malin in *William Faulkner: An Interpretation* (Stanford: Stanford University Press, 1957), pp. 37–38, believes Emily is the victim of self-repressed sexuality and, therefore, becomes masculinized. Faulkner, who dislikes masculine women, thus has an opportunity to analyze her necrophilia. Elmo Howell in "A Note on Faulkner's Emily as a Tragic Heroine,"

Serif, 2 (1966), 13–15, argues that if Emily is to be a tragic heroine, she cannot be a necrophiliac, nor can she kill Homer from such a petty motive as revenge. We have no indication that a break with Homer is imminent when he disappears. Therefore, the murder is a victory of the spirit over the body. Convinced that the affair is immoral, she kills Homer and keeps the body in an act of expiation. Faulkner's own comments do little to clarify matters. As quoted in Gwynn and Blotner's *Faulkner in the University* (Charlottesville: Univ. of Virginia Press, 1959), p. 58, he says in a March 1957 interview that Emily realized she had broken the law of her tradition and that her life was wrecked. She murdered to expiate her crime. In April, answering a question about the title, he says that she was a poor woman whose father was cruel and whose lover was about to desert her. She had to kill him to keep him (pp. 87–88). In May, asked about his inspiration, he replied that her natural emotions had been denied by her father who treated her as a servant, that all she wanted was "to be loved and to love" (p. 185). Earlier at Nagano, he was asked whether or not he liked Emily. He answered, "I feel sorry for Emily's tragedy; her tragedy was, she was an only child, an only daughter. At the time when she could have found a husband, could have had a life of her own, there was probably some one, her father, who said, "No, you must stay here and take care of me." And then when she found a man, she had had no experience in people. She picked out probably a bad one, who was about to desert her. And when she lost him, she could see that for her that was the end of life, there was nothing left, except to grow older, alone, solitary; she had had something and she wanted to keep it, which is bad—to go to any length to keep something; but I pity Emily. I don't know whether I would have liked her or not, I might have been afraid of her. Not of her but of anyone who had suffered, had been warped, as her life had probably been warped by a selfish father." (Robert Jelliffe, *Faulkner at Nagano* [Tokyo: Kenkyusha Ltd., 1956], pp. 70–71.) All of the above except Allen, O'Connor, Howell, and *Faulkner at Nagano* are reprinted in the Inge casebook.

⁴ William Faulkner, *The Collected Stories* (New York: Random House, Inc., 1950), p. 119. Page numbers appearing in the text are from this edition.

⁵ In a 1956 interview with Jean Stein, *Paris Review,* 12 (Spring 1956), 30, Faulkner says that "the short story is the most demanding form after poetry." In *Faulkner in the University,* p. 207, he says in a June 1957 interview, "In a short story that's next to the poem, almost every word has got to be almost exactly right . . . because it demands a nearer absolute exactitude. You have less room to be slovenly and careless. There's less room in it for trash. In poetry, of course, there's no room at all for trash. It's got to be absolutely impeccable, absolutely perfect."

⁶ *Faulkner in the University,* p. 59.

GEORGE L. DILLON

Styles of Reading

One of the things readers do with stories is to talk about them. These stories have not said it all, and readers derive evident pleasure from completing them, commenting on them, making them their own in various ways. Christine Brooke-Rose has recently called attention to the strategic incompleteness of good stories—spelling everything out treats the reader as stupid—and has suggested a classification of stories according to the tasks they leave to readers, or in which they entangle readers (Brooke-Rose 1980: 120–148). If we look at actual, published discussions of a story, however, we find no two of them answering the same set of questions, which suggests that we should look for questions (pre)inscribed in the reader as well as the text—the text, it is a matter of fact, has not very narrowly constrained the set of questions the readers have posed. As soon as we raise the matter of the actual performance of readers, however, we encounter a plethora of variables, and it has become something of a fashion in discussions of reading to enumerate them, often, it seems, to frighten scholars back to the study of narrative competence and the way texts constrain, or should constrain interpretations. Here, for example, is the list of Gerald Prince, a theorist who, though a strong believer in narrative competence, is a sceptic about the study of narrative performance:

> Of course, a given reader may be very tired or not at all, very young or very old, in a good mood or in a bad one; he may have a very good or a very deficient memory, a very great or very limited capacity for decentration, a considerable or moderate attention span; he may be a more or less experienced reader; he may be reading the text for the first, second, or tenth time; he may find the sentences and situations presented more or less familiar; he may want to read for fun or out of a sense of duty; he may show particular interest in the language, the plot, the characters, or the symbolism; he may hold one set of beliefs or another; and so on. In other words, his physiological, psychological, and sociological conditioning, his predispositions, feelings, and needs may vary greatly and so may his reading: his knowledge, his interests, and his aims determine to a certain extent the conventions, assumptions, and presuppositions he takes to underlie the text, the kinds of connections he is particularly interested in making, the questions he chooses to ask, and the answers he brings to them. (1980:229)

Barbara Herrnstein Smith offers a similar list of factors that may influence how and how much a reader may construct of the "chronology of events" which underlies a narrative (Smith 1980:213–236). If we are concerned with how people actually do read stories, however, these lists outline an area for research. Idiosyncratic variation may be a bogeyman; on the other hand, it may pose serious threats to communication, requiring rigorous methodological rules and the exercise of institutional authority. Perhaps there are underlying regularities which *in fact* shape readers' performances; perhaps there are none. In this article, I will examine readings of Faulkner's "A Rose for Emily," and focus initially on one area of variation—the answers readers have given to questions about the chronological sequence, or "event chain," of the story—to see how wild the variation is and what hope there may be of identifying regularities of performance.

One reason for focusing on event chains is that these have been among the most intensively studied of the many aspects of story comprehension. The term *event chain* is being used in a slightly technical way to refer to a graph connecting material in a story as events and causes of events, actions and motives of actions, enablements of events or actions, responses to events or actions and consequences of these. Readers employ two basic operations in building event chains: connection and inference. No story I know of spells out all of the terms and connections in an event chain (Miss Emily's motive for murdering Homer Barron, for example, is left for the reader to infer, as is the connection of the arsenic to the murder), and a story that did spell them all out would treat the reader as inconceivably stupid. Two distinctions are in order here: event chains are not precisely chronological, though I think they do correspond closely to what Professor Smith means by chronological sequences, that is, a certain sequentiality is implicit in the notions of motive, action, cause, response, and consequence, but not necessarily clock or calendar time, nor do pieces of the overall chain have to be strictly ordered; different sequences may overlap. This point is quite clear in regard to "A Rose for Emily": it seems possible to establish a chronology of the story that orders all of its major incidents, though it is very difficult to do so,[1] and it is not necessary to have worked out such a time scheme in order to get major portions of the event chain straight. Second, event chains are not "plots" in the sense defined by story grammars, nor in the traditional "rising-falling" interpretation.[2] That is, they are shapeless and open-ended; they do not account for any sense of beginning, climax, or conclusion. I assume that such structures can be fitted over them, or parts of the chains explained in terms of these notions—or not, as the reader desires. Hence event chains are part of the comprehension of all narratives; indeed, of all happenings, not just stories. One final proviso—we probably should not speak of "the event chain" but of "event chaining," since what a reader infers and connects, and how far he or she carries some sequence, is the reader's choice.

When we survey the published criticism of "A Rose for Emily," we find a large and bewildering array of questions about the event chain that have been answered. These include:

1. Why weren't there suitable suitors for Emily?

2. How does Emily respond to being denied suitors?

3. Why does Emily take up with Homer Barron?

4. What happened when he left? Did he abandon her? Why did he come back?

5. Why did she kill him?

6. Why did the smell disappear after only one week?

7. What did Miss Emily think of the men scattering lime around her house?

8. How did the hair come to be on the pillow? How much hair is a *strand*?

9. What was her relationship to Tobe?

10. Did she lie beside the corpse? How often, for what period of years?

11. Why did she not leave the house for the last decade of her life?

12. Did she not know Colonel Sartoris had been dead ten years when she faced down the Aldermen?

13. How crazy was she (unable to distinguish fantasy from reality)?

14. Why does she allow so much dust in her house?

There is also one question that has been asked but not answered, as far as I know: What transpired when the Baptist minister visited her? As the specialists in story comprehension have noted, once we realize that a Story Comprehender must have the power to carry out inferences in order to comprehend even the simplest story and give it that power, the problem becomes one of limiting the inferences drawn to some "relevant" subset of the possible ones. William Warren, David Nicholas, and Tom Trabasso suggest a first approximation of "relevance" as some inference that advances the main story line (Warren et al. 1979), but it is not clear how to apply this principle to the fourteen questions and answers, since every one of those questions was answered by at least one critic who felt the answer was relevant to the interpretation of the story—relevant to determining her motives, naming her actions, and so on. Of course, some of these event-chain inferences are stimulated by the particular interpretation a critic is putting forth, but there does not seem to be any basis on which to separate those inferences that are made independent of an interpretation from those which are not; event chaining is not an autonomous activity, but rather is subject to varying degrees of top-down guidance. People do not agree on the story to then disagree on the interpretation. It is simply not true that, as Wolfgang Iser claims, "On the level of plot, then, there is a high degree of intersubjective consensus," with subjective variation arising at the level of significance (Iser 1978: 123).[3] In fact, when we look at the list of questions that have been answered, the construction of event chains seems wildly unconstrained.

If we look at whole readings, however, some system and pattern does emerge. There are two surveys of the criticism of this story, and both find it fairly easy to group the readings into three classes (though the classes are somewhat differently defined; see Holland 1975:21–24; Perry 1979:62–63, et passim). We could group the readings according to what one might call "approaches," suggesting by that term some set of general questions readers taking a particular approach tend to pose of texts they read. This notion can be pushed in two, opposite directions. Taking it one way, we could argue that the variation considered so far does not directly reflect the way readers read but the way critics write about stories when they have an eye toward publication; the facts presented so far pose questions for the sociology of literature, or the history of literary criticism, not for the theory of reading. Taken the other way, these approaches could be viewed as personal styles or preferences in reading that happen to have acquired some public sanction. We generally have some style of reading before we know much about "approaches," after all, though we may learn other questions to ask when we study literature. In any case, one must have learned the approach in order to use it, so an approach is to some degree part of the cognitive equipment of a reader who employs it, however imperfectly integrated into his other modes of thinking it may be. Some light on the matter is shed, I think, by the very copious transcripts of interviews with undergraduate English majors about "A Rose for Emily" published by Norman Holland in *Five Readers Reading* (1975).

Holland's students also show three distinct approaches, and these approaches match up with the types of approaches in the published criticism. Though the student subjects may have gotten some leads from the criticism and they may be editing their responses to various degrees when presenting them to Professor Holland, they do seem to be giving what they feel are their own responses and to be responding in somewhat original—but consistent—ways to his questions. Also, because Holland has them talk about three stories, they could not have been greatly influenced by any one piece of published criticism, and indeed, the criticism they chose to be influenced by as much reflects their cognitive styles as it determines them. Holland's study strongly suggests that there are styles of reading stories, characteristic ways that readers interrogate texts, and that the "approaches" in the criticism are indeed rooted in the critics' own styles of reading and appeal to like-minded readers. I will illustrate this correspondence for three basic styles, which I will call the Character-Action-Moral (CAM) style, the Digger for Secrets style, and the Anthropologist style.

The CAM style differs markedly from the other two in treating the meaning (or significance) as more or less evident in the story: the reader makes the text his own, and makes the reading more apparent, by elaborating the event chain in the direction of the main character's traits, motives, thoughts, responses, and choices. To do this, CAM readers treat the world of the text as an extension or portion of the real world, the characters as real persons, so that we will recognize the experience of characters as being like our own experience; hence it can be understood or explained just as we would understand our own experience. Thus, the inferences they draw are based on commonsense notions of the way the world is, people are, etc. The other two styles appropriate the text not by immersion, but by analytic distance, probing and abstracting behind what is said; they assume that the world of the text is an edited version of our world—a *structure* rather than a glimpse or fragment. The CAM reader works by amalgamating the story into the body of his own beliefs and practical axioms about how life is or should be, the analytic styles by postulating the otherness or strangeness of the text.

The standard CAM reading contains lists of traits that account for the actions of the main character in a straightforward evaluative fashion (Brooks and Warren [1948:409–414]: "What is Miss Emily like? What are the mainsprings of her character?" p. 411). The actions are assumed to be pointers toward relatively permanent and pervasive characteristics, and one often finds "it could be otherwise" speculations in CAM readings (e.g., "A Rose for Emily" could have had a happy outcome if Homer Barron had been a marrying man—West [1973:192–198]; if another man had proposed to Emily after she finished with Homer, she would have declined the offer because she felt herself already married—Sam, in Holland [1975:138–139]). That is, the notion of character seems to presuppose the freedom of individuals to choose their responses to their situations, and stories like "A Rose for Emily" are treated as collisions between characters and situations—as *tragedies,* in the traditional Butcher/Bradley sense:

> Perhaps the horrible and the admirable aspects of Miss Emily's final deed arise from the same basic fact of her character: she insists on meeting the world on her own terms. She never cringes, she never begs for sympathy, she refuses to shrink into an amiable old maid, she never accepts the community's ordinary judgments or values. This independence of spirit and pride can, and does in her case, twist the individual into a sort of monster, but, at the same time, this refusal to accept the hero values carries with it a dignity and courage (Brooks and Warren, p. 413).

(Brooks and Warren later suggest Lear and Hamlet as parallels, but their language suggests Richard III as closer to hand.) We can see here the way the common notion of tragedy directs the reading toward character analysis; it also introduces three other questions, namely, those of awareness, tragic flaw, and moral. The evoking or constructing of character seems to lead directly to inference on the character's thoughts. When done naïvely, the results are fairly obtrusive, as when Holland's Sam says Emily has an awareness that "things were moving on, that things were changing, and yet, a similar awareness that she was unable to change along with them" (p. 137). More subtle is a partial merging of reader's and character's points of view. The reader talks about the character in terms the character himself might use: "She lost her honor, and what else could she do but keep him [Homer] forever, make him hers in the only way she possibly could?" (Sam, p. 137). This is remarkably similar to statements in the published readings of Brooks and Warren and West:

> Emily's world, however, continues to be the Past (in its extreme form it is death), and when she is threatened with desertion and disgrace, she not only takes refuge in that world, but she also takes Homer with her, in the only manner possible (West, p. 195).

> She would marry the common laborer, Homer Barron, let the community think what it would. She would not be jilted. And she would hold him as a lover. But it would all be on her own terms (Brooks and Warren, pp. 413–414).

> From the moment that she realizes that he will desert her, tradition becomes magnified out of all proportion to life and death, and she conducts herself as though Homer really had been faithful—as though this view represented reality (West, pp. 195–196).

This construction of an inner logic for the character is essential to the drawing of the moral: once we have realized the character's viewpoint, we can see the fatal flaw, the impulses or tendencies in ourselves that we should not give in to. If this immersion and identification with the character (which is plainly the identification of the character with the reader, in terms of himself) fails, then the story is, as Lionel Trilling concluded of "A Rose for Emily," without larger human import (1931:491–492). In this story, the CAM reader must direct his attention away from the details that suggest Miss Emily is not "like us" (above all, the questions about sleeping next to the corpse). The published critics can simply maintain silence on the question; Holland raised it, however, in his interviews, and Sam simply refused to pursue it. Even lines of inference that would attribute dark or complex motives are avoided or treated as normal. In regard to question (2) (Why Homer?), West discreetly suggests the usual, healthy, sexual urges, without considering that Homer is the utter subversion of Grierson hauteur and a most improbable candidate for a husband, that Emily flaunts her involvement, and so on. It is to Sam's credit that he records this as a "gap" in the story (according to his characterization of her as a tragic heroine).

Sam, in fact, has difficulty establishing a basic identification in the other two stories he read. In the case of Fitzgerald's "Winter Dreams," he finds Dexter's idealizing of Judy Jones a bit silly, concludes that neither that idealizing nor his actions reflect a tragic flaw, and complains that the moral to be drawn is obvious and banal: "We're taught this lesson through every damn novel, you know. . . . The lesson of the past, the knowledge, the realization in every hero throughout the damn thing that it cannot be retraced, that you try ceaselessly to recapture the past and that it forever eludes you" (p. 309). The story lavishly traces Dexter's thoughts, and it seems simply not to have left Sam enough of the kinds of questions he likes to answer. Sam does engage in some "it could have been otherwise" speculation and elaborates certain details of Judy's "fall" into housewifery, but on the whole, the story is too familiar and too explicit for him to take a great interest in it. He has even greater difficulty with Hemingway's "The Battler." Although he at first praises the story because he thinks "it's a valuable look at Nick Adams" (p. 319), he also complains that "we don't get much into Nick's mind" (p. 326)—which is certainly true, and a bit of an enigma if you are looking for meaning in terms of the impact of Nick's experience on him. Sam cannot find a plot with a significant, life-altering decision in it, and he says, "I don't know what it's doing if it's not doing symbolic things" (p. 319). And obviously, Sam's style of reading doesn't have much use for symbolism, since symbolism is mainly used to get beyond, behind, or beneath the conscious awareness that characters have of the reasons and implications of their actions. His two comments on symbolic or emblematic significance of details in "A Rose for Emily" point right back to the characters and their relationships: Her house represents "her whole way of life" (p. 136) and the tableau of Emily's father standing on the porch with a horsewhip driving away suitors symbolizes "the kind of relationship they had" (p. 137). Sam's wording is pedestrian, but Brooks and Warren and West say essentially the same thing (West, p. 193; Brooks and Warren, p. 411).

In sum, then, the CAM style is not afraid to state the obvious; it does not try to be ingenious or clever, but solid and useful; it does not assume the author is fashioning puzzles for us to solve, or playing tricks on us. The story conceals nothing—it is merely, of necessity, incomplete. For Diggers for Secrets, however, the story enwraps secrets, the narrator hides them—much as Miss Emily, and the narrator, conceal the body of Homer Barron—and the reader must uncover them. The title of Edward Stone's *A Certain Morbidness* suggests how he will read "A Rose for Emily." Diggers for Secrets expect narrators to screen us from the "reality,"

> But when, during her early spinsterhood, her father dies and she refuses for three days to hand his putrefying body over for burial, we are shocked by this irrational action, even though in keeping with his standpoint of noncommitment Faulkner tries to minimize it ("We remembered all the young men her father had driven away, and we knew that with nothing left, she would have to cling to that which had robbed her, as people will") (Stone 1969:96).

and expect the author only to give us clues:

> For Faulkner, so far from withholding all clues to Homer Barron's whereabouts, scatters them with a precise prodigality; since his is a story primarily of character, it is to his purpose to saturate our awareness of Miss Emily's abnormality as he goes, so that the last six shocking words merely put the final touch on that purpose (p. 65).

Sebastian, who is Holland's Digger, also comments on the evenhandedness of the narrator, whom he describes as switching sides (p. 177), and he too finds the maxim about holding on to that which robbed her a screen rather than an explanation: "Shouldn't have put that in, Bill," he says (p. 186). He even proposes to see through the author: "I wanted to see what unconscious things he would reveal about the South" (p. 186).

When Diggers for Secrets explain the psychology of characters, they employ the categories of depth and abnormal psychology (Stone even quotes Kraft-Ebbing's *Psychopathia Sexualis*) and frequently "diagnose" motives the characters would not be aware of and in terms they might well not accept. Sebastian uses the terms *sexuality, obsession,* and *necrophilia* heavily and confidently, but he still falls short, in eloquence at least, of Irving Malin and Edward Stone:

> Her passionate, almost sexual relationship with her dead father forces her to distrust the living body of Homer and to kill him so that he will resemble the dead father she can never forget.

> Not only does this obsessed spinster continue for some years to share a marriage bed with the body of the man she poisoned—she evidently derives either erotic gratification or spiritual sustenance (both?) from these ghastly nuptials. She becomes, in short, a necrophile or a veritable saprophytic organism; for we learn that the "slender figure in white" that was the young

> Miss Emily becomes, as though with the middle-aged propriety that the marriage customarily brings, fat! (Stone 1969:96).

Notice the assurance with which the "sleeping" questions are answered; Malin seems to ignore the dust on the bed. In a similar vein, Sebastian draws numerous inferences about the Negro servant Tobe's complicity in Emily's crime, about her "affair" with Homer, about the details of her sleeping with his corpse (how can a woman perform an act of necrophilia on a man?), and so on.

Symbolism being a ready avenue to non-obvious meanings, these readers find symbolic significances and secrets in details that the CAM readers either pass over or handle prosaically: Miss Emily's house for Stone is an isolated fortress, a forbidden, majestic stronghold; for Malin, Homer Barron represents "wild virility" (compare West's "earthiness"); for Sebastian, the title is richly ironic, "an unforgiveable irony in one sense: 'A Rose by any other name would not smell half as sweet!' There's not much sweetness about *her* rose. So I think the title refers to the decomposition of living matter, and so I take it ironically" (p. 182). Lest this seem jejune, note should be taken that William T. Going suggested this significance in *The Explicator* (1958, item 27). One expects such ironies from an author presumed to conceal.

An interesting feature of "A Rose for Emily" is that it contains not only a literal hidden secret (which Sebastian objects to as a bit too overt) but a "reader" as well (the narrator). That is, people who habitually look for the dirty reality behind appearances are open to the charge of prurience, a charge that would be easy to level at these readers, and one that the story conveniently allows us to displace onto the narrator ("the community") instead. So the taint of corruption spreads to the town, all these readers say, but, of course, not to *us*.[4] Thus in a sense, the abnormal becomes normal, and the story acquires the universality that raises it from case history to literature. The search for the abnormal and perverse finally leads back to the unacknowledged parts of our selves.

One would suppose that Diggers for Secrets would never be at a loss for things to discover in a story, but this is not the case, at least for Sebastian, who found "Winter Dreams" and "The Battler" less to his taste. In the case of "Winter Dreams," the illusion to be penetrated seems too obvious (Dexter's romanticizing of Judy Jones); in the case of "The Battler," he pursues many symbolic possibilities and explores the suggestion of homosexual undercurrents, but is dissatisfied because he can conclude nothing; the story may be rich in depths, but they do not converge as a secret to be discovered.

In short, he plays detective with the text, and wants to know when he has won the game. Other Diggers are less demanding, and seem to assume that if they have dug it up, it must be a secret. Philip Young's lead to his discussion of "The Battler" promises things of darkness if not secrets:

> People who complain about the sordid nature of many of Hemingway's stories seldom if ever cite this one, perhaps because the unpleasantness is more in the undertones and in things not said than in the outer events, which, though not happy, are not entirely extraordinary in our time. But if the subtleties are drawn out and examined, "The Battler" is as unpleasant as anything its author ever wrote (see Johnson 1948, item 45; and the other references cited in the footnote in Perry 1979:346).

One should not suppose that Diggers for Secrets are exclusively attuned to tabooed "realities"—Stone detects a reference to a Yankee general who raided Mississippi in the Civil War in the name *Grierson*—but it is reasonable to expect them to be there, and touched indirectly, in literature. The reader then plays beat-the-censor with the author.

Though the Diggers for Secrets make use of abstractive codes that explain what is going on in the story, their interest in "what's really going on" does, as we have seen, lead to inferences elaborating the event chain. The third group, the Anthropologists, have much less to say about events than either of the first two groups. Their interest, rather, is in identifying the cultural norms and values that explain what characters indisputably do and say. Like Diggers for Secrets, these readers go beneath the surface and state things that are implicit and not said, though what they bring out is not a secret, but the general principles and values which the story illustrates as an example. To some degree, early readings that talk of a conflict in "A Rose for Emily" between the North and the South, or old versus new South, outline this approach, but these readings tended to be brief and schematic, as if critics were not willing to reopen old wounds (Gwynn and Blotner 1965: 47–48). And, too, Faulkner was on record as not intending such an interpretation.[5] When a reader is especially engaged in the critique of the norms and values of American society, however, the story takes on interest as an extended exemplum. Thus the two instances of this style of reading, Holland's Shep and Judith Fetterley, are both radicals. For Shep, who is Holland's example of a sixties radical, the characters and events of the story exemplify forces of social struggle—class struggle, racial struggle, and above all the struggle between true and false values. Thus he says Emily's father represents the old code, the dead hand of the past; Homer Barron represents the forces of aimless technology; Emily herself was, he says, "perpetuating the same ethos in which her father lived" (p. 61); "In a way, Miss Emily is a descendant of the culture hero, except that she's a descendant of the culture hero in his waning phase" (p. 166); "They had a very rigid formal code and it was perhaps very much a dead code by the time she got her hands on it, but it represented something which the new people weren't able to offer an adequate substitute for" (p. 161). Proceeding at such a lofty plane, he is fairly indifferent to the detailed goings-on of the event chain, though he does infer Emily's response to the lime-scattering incident—namely, scorn for the men—and he is willing to speculate under Holland's urging. He offers two motives for the murder, first, simple revenge, to keep him from leaving her; but he also evolves a second, mythic explanation, which I quote at some length:

> She can reverse the social decay process by putting her lover, representative of all of them ["the newcomers"] through a physical decay process and coming to relish the sight. This would also give some sort of, quote, explanation, unquote, for her necrophilic hangups. The fact that she wanted her father's body around to [. . .] preserve it from decay—she was denying the end of the line thing symbolized by putting it underground and letting the earth have it (p. 171).

Though he judges that this attempt failed:

> She feels personally that with Homer she managed to offset the decay process around her and, for that matter, within her, as she represents the tradition [. . .] she doesn't really do it. Becoming "Barron," she didn't prevail in the way that she thought she had. For her, maybe, she went to the grave triumphant, but for everyone else, she went to the grave dead. I think that's the judgment that has to be made, after all. Aw, hell—drive through Jefferson, Mississippi, Oxford, Mississippi, and you can see this judgment has to be made (p. 174).

So there is a double or triple pattern of explanation here—commonsense psychology (she wanted revenge), operation of social forces, and mythic patterns; these explanations seem somewhat detached from each other and so the reading is not completely totalized.

If Shep is an example of a sixties radical, then Judith Fetterley, in her book *The Resisting Reader* (1978), represents a kind of seventies version of the same basic style of reading. Fetterley focuses on stating the social norms and codes that explain the events of the story—there is very little in the way of constructive activity of motives, actions, responses, and consequences, except for a brief discussion of the lime-scattering incident. She also offers two motives for the murder: first, that Emily murdered Homer because she had to have a man (thus illustrating the brainwashing of the code), but she also offers the following symbolic/mythic account:

> Having been consumed by her father, Emily in turn feeds off Homer Barron, becoming, after his death, suspiciously fat. Or, to put it another way, it is as if, after her father's death, she has reversed his act of incorporating her by incorporating and becoming him, metamorphosed from the slender figure in white to the obese figure in black whose hair is "a vigorous iron-gray, like the hair of an active man." She has taken into herself the violence in him which thwarted her and has reenacted it upon Homer Barron (1978:42–43).

On first reading, this seems very much like Stone's celebration of Faulkner's "ghoulish evolution" of the gothic, but on closer examination, the passage is really suggesting a crude form of retributive justice, a pointed, if lurid, warning to the upholders of patriarchy. It is striking that the same elementary operations—*connecting* her growing fat to Homer's murder and *inferring* a causal link—result in such different explanations.

Like Shep, Fetterley makes heavy use of symbolic interpretation and the logic of example: Emily's confinement by her father represents confinement of women by patriarchy; the remission of taxes signifies continued dependence of women on men; the men's treatment of her, and her ability to buffalo them and commit murder without punishment, are explained in terms of the code of the "lady" who is assumed to be out of touch with reality, and must be kept so; Emily represents the town itself, and in discovering her nature, they discover their own. The focus of Fetterley's interest is in flushing the codes out of hiding and explaining what happens in terms of them, though it is not a totalizing reading in that she doesn't claim to have explained everything in the story in terms of the codes; this treatment represents the extreme of abstraction away from the events and surface of the story toward allegory and parable. That's what it means to be a Resisting Reader: to refuse to give yourself to the work, to accept any of its givens— and in fact, to bring precisely those axioms into question.

Clearly, then, these three styles or approaches are asking different questions of the text, and constructing what are to various degrees different stories in the course of answering them. We may think of them as concentrating their attentions on different codes in the Barthian sense: The CAM style is oriented toward the proairetic code, the Digger style toward the hermeneutic code, and the Anthropologist toward the referential code (cultural norms). I do not have any evidence for styles especially concentrated on the semic or symbolic codes, and, while these three styles surely do not exhaust the possibilities,[6] it seems unlikely that "semic" or "symbolic" styles will turn up. Semic (naming, categorizing, schematizing) and symbolic moves are scattered over the three styles we have considered and are deployed in different ways in each style. Similarly, I don't think we should expect to find a structuralist style as such: the basic moves of structural analysis (finding contrasting groups and repetitions of patterns) are used by CAM readers as well as by the more analytically inclined; the latter readers, however, are more likely to come up with non-obvious mythic or psychoanalytic patterns. In fact, these parallels perhaps should be taken as a glimmering of "objectivity" (or intersubjective consensus) about the text: Readers predisposed to a certain style of reading will, when faced with the same text, come up with some very similar stories along with some very similar explanations.

Second, and lastly, the notion that these styles are, or can become, general patterns of thinking, rather than a learned decorum of literary criticism, seems to derive support from the consideration that we also exhibit differences of styles in thinking about real people and events. We think of ourselves and others as conscious, moral agents shaping our destinies in situations benign and hostile, but also as mysteries to ourselves and others, and/or as enacting typical social roles and attitudes. There is some basis for concluding that we understand literature and life in the same or similar ways, and that some of the ways we read literature will be applied in reading others of life's texts.

REFERENCES

Brooke-Rose, Christine, 1980. "The Readerhood of Man," in: Susan R. Suleiman and Inge Crosman, eds. *The Reader in the Text* (Princeton: Princeton UP).

Brooks, Cleanth and Robert Penn Warren, 1948. *Understanding Fiction* (New York: F. S. Crofts).

Fetterley, Judith, 1978. *The Resisting Reader* (Bloomington & London: Indiana UP).

Going, William T., 1958. "Chronology in Teaching 'A Rose for Emily,'" *Exercise Exchange* 5, 8–11.

Gwynn, Frederick and Joseph L. Blotner, 1965. *Faulkner in the University* (New York: Vintage Books).

Hendricks, William O., 1977. "'A Rose for Emily': A Syntagmatic Analysis," *PTL* 2, 257–295.

Holland, Norman, 1975. *Five Readers Reading* (New Haven: Yale UP).

Iser, Wolfgang, 1978. *The Act of Reading* (Baltimore, Md.: Johns Hopkins UP).

Johnson, C. W. M., 1948. "Faulkner's 'A Rose for Emily.'" *Explicator* 6, item 45.

Malin, Irving, 1957. *William Faulkner: An Interpretation* (Palo Alto: Stanford UP).

McGlynn, Paul D., 1969. "The Chronology of 'A Rose for Emily.'" *Studies in Short Fiction* 6, 461–462.

Nebeker, Helen E., 1971. "Chronology Revisited," *Studies in Short Fiction* 8, 471–473.

Perry, Menakhem, 1979. "Literary Dynamics: How the Order of a Text Creates Its Meanings," *Poetics Today* 1:1–2.

Prince, Gerald, 1980. "Notes on the Text as Reader," in Susan R. Suleiman and Inge Crosman, eds. *The Reader in the Text* (Princeton: Princeton UP).

Smith, Barbara Herrnstein, 1980. "Narrative Versions, Narrative Theories," *Critical Inquiry* 7.

Stone, Edward, 1969. *A Certain Morbidness* (Carbondale: Southern Illinois UP).

Sullivan, Ruth, 1971. "The Narrator in 'A Rose for Emily,'" *Journal of Narrative Technique* 1, 159–178.

Trilling, Lionel, 1931. "Mr. Faulkner's World," *The Nation*, Nov. 4, 491–492.

Warren, William H., David W. Nicholas and Tom Trabasso, 1979. "Event Chains and Inferences in Understanding Narratives," in: Roy O. Freedle, ed. *New Directions in Discourse Processing* (Norwood, N.J.: Ablex Publishing).

Woodward, Robert W., 1966. "The Chronology of 'A Rose for Emily,'" *Exercise Exchange* 13, 17–19.

NOTES

[1]   At least five chronologies have appeared in print, all differing: Going (1958:8–11); Woodward (1966:17–19); McGlynn (1969:461–462); Nebeker (1971:471–473); and Perry (1979:35–63, 311–361).

[2]   There is a lengthy discussion of the story structure of "A Rose for Emily" in Hendricks (1977:257–295).

[3]   Iser's definition of *significance* as "the reader's absorption of the meaning into his own existence" (151) leaves us in need of an intermediate term between it and *plot* (event chains)—something like *explanation,* which is constructed to account for events (e.g., in terms of character traits, maxims of behavior, mythic patterns, etc.) but which is not necessarily the amalgamation of the story into the reader's subjectivity. For one thing, explanation need not be evaluative. I am using *interpretation* in a broad sense here to mean the reader's commentary minus any plot summary, though even the latter is usually tailored to fit the commentary.

[4]   For Ruth Sullivan, however, the narrator is a prying, probing voyeur, and so are we readers (1971:159–178).

[5]   There is one style which I find attested only in Holland's interviews (and in some of the papers of David Bleich's students), that we might call the Visualizer style, the style of Holland's Sandra, whose comments on all three stories are strongly weighted to descriptions of characters' expressions and feelings, decors and other physical details and commentary on the suitability of words, images, and tonal effects in the narration. This is perhaps the most surface- or craft-conscious of the styles, and the reason it does not appear in the published readings is that it is more a style of appreciation than explanation, or, to put it another way,

it is more concerned with explaining the details of the style and presentation ("discourse" in Seymour Chatman's terminology) than with the story. Academic criticism of fiction, it appears, has been concerned with stories, not discourse.

⁶ Holland of course would explain these consistencies in terms of basic, immutable personality themes (or styles), but I do not think we need to accept this grounding of cognitive styles in deeper, unconscious entities. Similarly, we can account for judgments of taste and lack of things to say in terms of matches and mismatches between cognitive styles of reading and texts; blocking and denial need not be involved. At issue really is the learnability of these approaches.

RUTH SULLIVAN

The Narrator in "A Rose For Emily"

I

Faulkner's well-read "A Rose for Emily" has been variously interpreted as a mere horror story about necrophilia and madness, as a story about the Old South contending with the New Order of the Post–Civil War era, as a tragic tale of a woman's noble but doomed effort to resist the forces of time, change, and death, and as a tale of the catastrophe that can result when someone allows illusion to become confused with reality.

Published criticism of this story shares two assumptions: that Miss Emily is its only important character and that she is somehow objectively presented; that is, that she can be analyzed as though she had an existence apart from the consciousness through whom Faulkner chose to reveal her. For "A Rose for Emily" is first-person narration, hence subject to the questions one usually puts in understanding such a story. For instance, who is the narrator and what is his relationship to the main action? Why did the author choose this particular narrator for this particular story?

All interpretations of "A Rose for Emily" tacitly or openly assume that its narrator has slight importance as a character, for his function is to be window pane or mirror upon the life of Miss Emily Grierson. One critic, Kenneth Payson Kempton, calls the narrator an "extreme of anonymity" who comes close to being totally objective. "A Rose for Emily" is

> a story whose narrator, some unidentified neighbor of the protagonist, stands at the farthest possible position from the heart of the story and still is within it . . . somebody who sees and hears what goes on without more than

average powers of interpretation and analysis and who is in touch with the surface facts only, and therefore whose discovery of what lies beneath the surface can pace the reader's discovery.[1]

In substance this statement is accurate because the narrator could be a neighbor, though necessarily more than one since the point of view is first person plural, "we," and is apparently an innocent eye. But it is not true that the narrator "is in touch with the surface facts only" because he[2] tells Miss Emily's story after the town has broken into her room and therefore after they all know her secrets. His apparent innocence is a story-teller's contrivance to heighten irony and suspense. Nor is it true that his "discovery of what lies beneath the surface can pace the reader's discovery" because the story is not told chronologically even within the flashback technique it uses. Finally, though the narrator is an "extreme of anonymity," it remains to be proven whether he is even approximately objective, for if objectivity is what Faulkner wanted, why did he not use a fly-on-the-wall point of view instead?

Only one critic who studies Faulkner's narrative technique in this story, Austin McGiffert Wright, casts slight doubt upon the objectivity of the narrator. He notes that sometimes statements in short stories sound so authoritative that the reader may be misled into accepting them as truths. For instance this from "A Rose for Emily": "Thus she passed from generation to generation dear, inescapable, impervious, tranquil, and perverse." Such statements, he says, "tell us something important about a character, [but] they also, like the fallible first-person-narrator previously noted, tend to omit something else of greater importance—something which can only be gathered through inference, from the story as a whole. In 'A Rose for Emily,' for example the adjectives 'dear, inescapable, impervious, tranquil, and perverse' apply only to the judgment of the town upon her before the secrets of Emily's private life are exposed."[3] Though Professor Wright does not draw further conclusions from this statement, it helps us draw our own, namely, that we would be naive readers indeed if we assumed the impartiality of the teller of this tale.

Brooks and Warren are the only critics to grant prominence to the narrator. "In order to make a case for the story as 'meaningful,' we shall have to tie Miss Emily's thoughts and actions back into the normal life of the community and establish some sort of relationship between them."[4] For the townspeople, Emily is not just an insane old lady but "a combination of idol and scapegoat for the community."[5] Nevertheless, Brooks and Warren treat the narrator as though he were a window pane.

I propose to demonstrate that we cannot understand Emily Grierson until we have understood the narrator, for he is the medium of consciousness through whom she is filtered; and that the narrator is an emotional participant in Miss Emily's life and therefore cannot be objective.

II

Who is the narrator? Not a single person because Faulkner uses a first-person plural point of view, "we"; that "we" is townspeople, but only such as are in position to watch Miss Emily constantly for fifty or sixty years: they are anonymous townspeople, for neither names nor sexes nor occupations are given or hinted at; and they seem to be naive watchers, for they speak as though they did not understand the meaning of the events at the time they occurred. Further, they are of indeterminate age. By details given in the story they are neither older nor younger nor of the same age as Miss Emily.[6]

The most significant action the narrator performs is watching. In fact we can talk about "A Rose for Emily" as a story about a woman watched for a long time by a narrator-group curious to know every detail of her appearance, conduct, family life, and environment. The story opens with an announcement about this curiosity: "When Miss Emily Grierson died, our whole town went to her funeral: the men through a sort of respectful affection for a fallen monument, the women *mostly out of curiosity to see the inside of her house*, which no one save an old man-servant—a combined gardener and cook—had seen in at least ten years" (emphasis added).[7] And it continues with example after example of this close scrutiny, from the description of her house as "an eyesore among eyesores" through the curious gaze around her parlor by the Board of Aldermen come to collect taxes, to the intense watching of her courtship by Homer Barron ("we began to *see* him and Miss Emily," "we sat back to *watch* developments," "that was the last we *saw* of Homer Barron," etc.), and finally to the curiosity at her funeral: "The Negro met the first of the ladies at the front door and let them in, with their hushed, sibilant voices and their *quick, curious glances . . .* ," and the curiosity which leads to discovery of the man's skeleton and the climactic sight: "then we *noticed* that in the second pillow was the indentation of a head. One of us lifted something from it, and leaning forward, that faint and invisible dust dry and acrid in the nostrils, we *saw* a long strand of iron-gray hair."

The town's curiosity about Miss Emily is stirred by respect, admiration, awe, and affection; but it is also and equally stirred by discomfort and revulsion. The pattern of this response to Miss Emily may be roughly charted:

curiosity is fairly consistent with this exception, that it grows unusually intense over Miss Emily's courtship by Homer Barron and over the contents of her locked bedroom. Affection and respect dominate the town's feeling for her through the death of her father; then discomfort and revulsion dominate from the Homer Barron period until beyond her death when they break into her room. The first faint evidence of the town's revulsion shows in the narrator's description of Miss Emily's house as an "eyesore among eyesores" and then in his first description of the living Miss Emily as

> a small, fat woman in black, with a thin gold chain descending to her waist and vanishing into her belt, leaning on an ebony cane with a tarnished gold head. Her skeleton was small and spare; perhaps that was why what would have been merely plumpness in another was obesity in her. She looked bloated, like a body long submerged in motionless water, and of that pallid hue. Her eyes, lost in the fatty ridges of her face, looked like two small pieces of coal pressed into a lump of dough. . . .

The next image is the putrid smell as of "a snake or a rat that nigger of hers killed in the yard." After the courtship and subsequent disappearance of Homer Barron, the narrator describes her as having "grown fat," then as scarcely human, sitting "like the carven torso of an idol in a niche," then as dead and buried, while in her bedchamber lie the decayed nightclothes and skeleton of her lover. The town is fond of Emily, but it is also repelled by her.[8]

The characteristics of the narrator-group as we have thus far adduced them are that it is an anonymous and once-naive group of townspeople who watch Miss Emily, aristocrat and town eccentric, with an intense and enduring (fifty- or sixty-year) curiosity. She rouses ambivalent feelings in this narrator-group, hence its story about her cannot be objective.

But these characteristics do not yet fully explain why Emily should mean so much to the narrator nor in what ways he distorts his presentations of her. Answers to these questions lie in an examination of the manner of the telling, for that manner will reveal some disturbing qualities of the teller.

III

"A Rose for Emily" is an uncomfortable story, not only because its subject is necrophilia hinted at and shockingly revealed but because we sense some unsavory qualities in the teller. For instance, his curiosity. Clearly it is active, for it allows Miss Emily no privacy at all except such as she can win for herself by isolation. Though one might counter that such interest is natural in ordinary folk captured by a public figure who is also unusually eccentric, nevertheless the narrator's curiosity goes far beyond the normal. He often aggressively intrudes into the intimate life of a harmless woman (harmless as far as he knew) and then reveals for public inspection that juicy gossip about her sexual life. For this, after all, is the main concern of that narrator. He wants to know not just what Miss Emily is doing, but what she is doing with Homer Barron and what is in her locked bedroom. And lest my reader accuse me of pan-sexualism here, let me remind him that whatever its theme, "A Rose for Emily" is a kind of mystery story whose plot turns on the discovery of the corpse of Homer Barron, preserved and embraced by the jilted spinster.

Sexual curiosity, then, drives the narrator. He is at times aggressive and even sadistic in his penetration into Miss Emily's house and affairs. The instrument of this penetration is not the phallus but the eyes. The narrator is a voyeur. The very structure of "A Rose for Emily" demonstrates this, for according to Floyd C. Watkins, Faulkner "divided the story into five parts and based them on *incidents of isolation and intrusion.*"[9] I quote Professor Watkins extensively now: "The contrast between Emily and the townspeople and between her home and its surroundings is carried out by *the invasions of her home* by the adherents of the New Order in the town." Each such contributes to the story's suspense, has its own crisis. The first invasion is that of the Aldermen come to collect her taxes, "the second part describes *two forced entrances into her isolation,* both of them caused by a death," Homer Barron's and her father's. "*The inviolability of Miss Emily's isolation* is maintained in the central division, Part Three, in which *no outsider enters her home.*" In Part Four there are two forced entries, those of the Baptist minister and the Alabama relations; in Part Five "the horde comes to bury a corpse, a Miss Emily no longer able to defy them."[10] As Professor Watkins sees it, then, Miss Emily is involved in defending herself against "invasions," "intrusion," and "forced entrances" by the New Order and the townspeople and this defense has something to do with her "isolation" and "inviolability"—phallic intrusion into Miss Emily's virginity (Professor Watkins, more subtle than I, does not use these terms). But since the purpose of these invasions is always in part to find out what is inside Miss Emily's house, to *see,* they are phallic in form but voyeuristic in nature.

Miss Emily's house is Miss Emily herself if we read symbolically. Faulkner seems to spend some effort on having us draw such an equation for the first thing he describes in Emily's story is not the lady but her house. Like Miss Emily it stands "lifting its stubborn and coquettish decay" alone amidst alien surroundings. When the town complains about the smell emanating from the house, the judge equates house and woman: "'Will you accuse a lady to her face of smelling bad?'" Miss Emily becomes a fallen woman, a fact foreshadowed in that initial description of where she lived, in a house that had "once been white . . . set on what had once been our most select street . . . lifting its stubborn and coquettish decay above the cotton wagons and the gasoline pumps—an eyesore among eyesores." The house, like Miss Emily, has fallen from purity and like Miss Emily it is an eyesore, for the immediately succeeding description has her looking like a bloated corpse.

If the house is symbol for Miss Emily's self, then the intrusions of the townspeople must be symbol for intrusions on Miss Emily's body and the climactic forced entry into her bedroom must be a symbolic rape—a rape performed upon a dead woman. The story opens with "when Miss Emily Grierson died" and continues with a description of an aggressive inquiry into her privacy that in effect performs upon the dead woman a kind of sexual exposure. Even while describing the living woman it makes her into a kind of corpse: "Her skeleton was small and spare; perhaps that was why what would have been merely plumpness in another was obesity in her. She looked bloated, like a body long submerged in motionless water, and of that pallid hue." Finally they can gratify a curiosity insatiable for fifty or sixty years but only upon a dead woman and then forcibly, violently. "They waited until Miss Emily was decently in the ground before they opened it." They force the door. "Already we knew that there was one room in that region above stairs which no one had seen in forty years, and which would have to be forced. . . . The violence of breaking down the door seemed to fill this room with pervading dust." To break into a woman's room is symbolically to rape her. To rape a dead woman is to perform necrophilia.

The revelation that now follows shocks us, causes vague anxieties and even such an effort to deny the evidence that has led some critics to say that "there is no evidence in the story that she lay in the bed with Homer Barron after the night she murdered him,"[11] or to assume that Miss Emily *placed* the strand of hair there.[12] But surely these are denials of the clear signs Faulkner leaves that Miss Emily slept for years next to the decaying body of the man she murdered.[13]

What causes the vague anxiety and shock this scene arouses is, of course, its gruesome perversion. But whose perversion? Miss Emily's to be sure, but also the narrator's—and the reader's. Every unnatural act performed by Miss Emily is performed in some fashion by the narrator, too, if not in the flesh then in deeds symbolically similar. Miss Emily kills and cohabits with her lover; the narrator symbolically rapes the dead spinster. Miss

Emily is an eccentric escapee of reality and a radical self-isolator, but the town's offenses against her are more severe than hers against them. They are peeping toms refusing her privacy. All these things the reader senses throughout the story but most intensely during its climax, for the narrator has hypnotized us into such close identification with him (his anonymity and persistent use of "we" and "you" encourage this identification) that we, too, become mental necrophiliacs and voyeurs. Now at the climax we are dragged against powerful inner resistance into witnessing something that stirs repressed memories or fantasies of the locked and forbidden bedroom in which a man and a woman are doing things we were curious but also fearful to know about. The climax of "A Rose for Emily" seems to reproduce such a buried fantasy, conceived by a sadistic narrator. For here the love-making in the forbidden chamber is deadly. The uncanniness of the scene derives from the fact that Faulkner has given us intercourse as it is understood by the child, as an assault of one partner upon the other with pain or death the necessary result. The twist here, though, is that usually if a child imagines the primal scene sadistically, he believes that it is the woman and not the man who is harmed. Not so for this watcher. He sees woman as man-destroyer.[14]

The uncanny effect of the final scene derives from the revival of yet another repressed fantasy, for behind the one of a sadistically conceived primal scene lies another about what one might find inside a woman's body. And the voyeur-narrator sees what childish imagination makes him see there: feces (the room is filled with dust and contains a rotted nightshirt and a decayed corpse); baby (the body); and penis (a man).[15]

Faulkner has carefully prepared his readers for this assault upon the dead woman, most clearly in the action of the Board of Aldermen who "broke open the cellar door and sprinkled lime there. . . ." Then, the townspeople speak of the Griersons as "high and mighty" and are pleased when Mr. Grierson left Miss Emily a pauper. "Now she too would know the old thrill and the old despair of a penny more or less." And after she has bought arsenic, they believe she will commit suicide. "So the next day we all said, 'She will kill herself'; and *we said it would be the best thing.*" The townspeople are fond of Miss Emily, they respect her and even stand in awe of her, but they are also repelled and somewhere beneath all these other feelings they harbor powerful aggressive wishes against her.

So far I have concentrated my discussion of the narrator on trying to demonstrate that "A Rose for Emily" is about a double emotional aberration, Miss Emily's and her storyteller's. The skeptical may call this interpretation into question by arguing that after all, actions and intentions are not in fact the same. Miss Emily (we are asked to believe) actually committed necrophilia, she is actually insane given as she is to denials of the great facts of human life like passage of time, loss of loved ones, decay, and death. But the narrator has not actually performed necrophilia; he has not raped a dead woman except by symbolic acts, and symbol is not deed or object. And while he may be a voyeur, the narrator is not insane.

All this is true, but we must keep in mind that the most significant function the narrator performs is to be medium of consciousness through whom Faulkner has us see Miss Emily. That medium is important less for what he does (though entering Miss Emily's bridal chamber is a significant act) than for what and how he sees and reports upon what he has seen. Now it makes a difference to our understanding of Emily Grierson if we perceive that the narrator who describes her is given to his own kinds of emotional aberrations, for then we must question how objective the telling medium can be.

IV

The narrator is not objective. He is dominated by pressing needs, desires, and fears that would render reports on the object of his emotional involvement unreliable. He is sometimes aggressive against Miss Emily because she has frustrated him in certain of the crucial but unspoken demands he makes upon her, one of which is that she gratify his sexual curiosity—she will not do it. As for what Miss Emily means to the narrator, why he should take her rather than someone else as his object of curiosity, that must be answered in two ways: on the manifest story level she is a high-born and eccentric citizen to curious neighbors. On this level the term "voyeur" to describe the narrator is inappropriate. On the latent level, she is a mother to a child.

This may sound absurd on first hearing, Miss Emily as a mother, the narrator as a child, for Miss Emily seems far from being a mother figure—she never married, had no children, lived alone, and took care of no one. And the narrator seems far from being a child—his age is indeterminate, hence there is no way of demonstrating that he is young enough to be her child, nor is there evidence that he is related to her by blood, that he depends upon her materially, or even that Miss Emily knew him so that she could be concerned about him.

But I am not saying the narrator is her child, only that he is a child—and not chronologically but psychically: his psychic development is infantile. Nor am I saying that Miss Emily is anyone's mother. She is a mother figure.

For reasons not given in the story the narrator makes Miss Emily assume this role.

More precisely, the narrator is not persons at all but an archaic consciousness (i.e., one dominated by infantile fixations) that Faulkner objectifies as persons in only two places in the story, once at the beginning when the narrator attends Miss Emily's funeral and at the end when he enters her bridal chamber. But otherwise the "we" disappears into the texture of the story. That "we" performs psychological and intellectual activities but no physical ones except watching and once entering Miss Emily's house. But this act is passive, for he goes in there primarily in order to see. If to these facts we add our remembrance that Faulkner gives the narrator neither face, sex, name, occupation, nor age, then this assertion that the narrator has only one dimension, a psychic one, should be convincing.

What remains to be proven now are the assertions that this perceiving medium is archaic and that it takes Miss Emily as mother figure.

V

Evidence that on some level the narrator is archaic consciousness may be found in the way Faulkner uses time in the story—time as theme and as structure. As theme, some critics see "A Rose for Emily" as making a statement about what happens to someone who denies the passage of time and hence denies such of its attendants as change, loss, decay, and death. For instance, Ray B. West says, "The principal contrast in William Faulkner's short story 'A Rose for Emily' is between past time and present time."[16] Miss Emily's retreat into the past is escape from facing the fact of desertion. "Emily's small room above stairs has become that timeless meadow. In it, the living Emily and the dead Homer have remained together as though not even death could separate them."[17] And she does conquer time, but only briefly, for "in its simplest sense, the story says that death conquers all."[18] Result of such denial must be insanity. And other critics see time as theme in that Miss Emily (as already stated) represents the Old Order in conflict with modern times. "One pattern that is most evident throughout the story is the analogy between Emily and the Old South."[19]

Time is important as structure, too, for Faulkner has the narrator perform such radical dislocations of chronology in telling Miss Emily's story that Wright calls his technique an "abandonment of chronology."[20] And Faulkner even leads one to suspect something so uncanny as the possibility that Miss Emily died (by dates given in the text) any time between 1934 and 1938, three to seven years after "A Rose for Emily" was copyrighted.[21]

A closer look throws this conjecture into question; nevertheless it might be instructive to examine Faulkner's handling of chronology and then to speculate on why he does it that way and why he should make time itself a theme.

Roughly the narrative technique of "A Rose for Emily" is flashback, for the story begins with Emily's burial and ends with the post-mortem events of breaking into her bridal chamber. The story between fills in her life from the earliest incident the narrator recounts about her (the father driving suitors away) until just after her death. The flashback has this rough form, that in Parts I and II the narrator swings us back deep into Miss Emily's past, and then in Parts III and IV moves almost consistently forward to her death. However, if we refine this broad pattern we notice the striking fact that the deep plunge back to Miss Emily's past performed in the first two parts is far from consistently backward-turning. The narrator veers radically backward and forward from event to event and even flashes backward and forward within individual events to record some related memories. For example, the story begins at the end of Miss Emily's life. It then goes *backward* to 1894 and sometime after her father's death when Colonel Sartoris has her taxes remitted; then *forward* from there to the next generation that demands those taxes; then *backward* to the smell incident thirty years earlier. Now the narrator's recording of that incident, of the one following it concerning the death of Emily's father, and of her courtship by Homer Barron twists chronology almost beyond recognition. First, the smell episode precedes the other two in the narrative, but in terms of Miss Emily's biography, it postdates her father's death and her courtship. Second and more remarkable is the way the narrator shifts from past to present to past during each episode. For instance in the smell episode—the narrator places the time as thirty years before the failure of the earlier, tax-collecting Board of Aldermen, two years after Emily's father's death, and "a short time" after Homer Barron deserted her.

This veering chronology in parts of the story makes the plot structure seem almost formless, for clearly events are linked by neither consecutive time periods (even if we proceed from events at the beginning of the flashback) nor by causality, for while the narrator is concerned with why Miss Emily killed and cohabited with her lover, he is equally concerned with what impact her life had upon his and upon that of the town. Nevertheless, time does structure "A Rose for Emily." Its pattern is not by chronology but by the emotional association one event bears to another in the narrator's consciousness. "A Rose for Emily" sounds like interior monologue, like a tale the narrator tells to himself but that we overhear, for the narrative pattern imitates the flux of normal thought; it is organized by feeling rather than by logic.

Now since this temporal structuring is performed by the narrator and since it is for him that time itself is an important issue, we may conclude that Faulkner is characterizing the narrator even as he is arranging plot and creating theme. That is, we may infer from the emotional structuring of the telling that the narrator is emotionally engaged with Miss Emily; we may infer from his radical temporal swings and his tendency to treat even very early events as equally vivid with more recent ones (i.e., the tendency to flatten time, to make past seem present) that he is speaking out of some deeply-engaged psychic level, for it is there in unconscious or preconscious mental life that past and present seem to merge, that the past remains peculiarly vivid and fully alive. Finally, his preoccupation with time itself, especially the past, is an appropriate preoccupation for a medium of consciousness so essentially infantile. We might at this point remember that Faulkner makes his narrator an innocent eye; *i.e.,* childlike in perception.

VI

The object of the childlike perception is Miss Emily; she is the narrator's mother-figure because only the real or surrogate mother could engage infantile feelings so deeply and enduringly. The narrator has been fascinated by Miss Emily for nearly sixty years; he clearly has various, powerful, and ambivalent emotions about her; and he has both idealized and degraded her beyond human limits. He sees her as godlike, defying all merely human laws, institutions, and relationships, for she will not pay taxes or allow numbers and a mailbox to be affixed to her house, she resists allowing her father to be buried, she does not even marry as normal people do. And she commits murder almost under the eyes of a town that (we feel) should have known eventually why she bought that arsenic. She takes human life and no human law stops or punishes her for it. Godlike, she lives in a "timeless meadow" for she also defies superhuman forces of time and death. And she is several times referred to as an angel and an idol: "her hair was cut short, making her look like a girl, with a vague resemblance to those *angels in colored church windows* sort of tragic and serene." "As they recrossed the lawn, a window that had been dark was lighted and Miss Emily sat in it, the light behind her, and her upright torso motionless as that of *an idol.*" "Now and then we would see her in one of the downstairs windows . . . like the carven torso of *an idol in a niche.* . . ." The children who take china-painting lessons "were sent to her with the same regularity and in the same spirit that they were sent *to church on Sundays* with a twenty-five-cent piece for the collection plate." The Griersons have always been "high and mighty," somehow above "the gross, teeming world" and now, disgraced because of her conduct with Homer Barron, she succumbs (they say) to a "touch of earthiness." It seems the town needs occasionally to bring her down from godhood to humanity. For instance when her father leaves her penniless, "they could pity Miss Emily. Being left alone, and a pauper, she had become humanized." But she never does become fully humanized and the town never loses its fear of her. She is always unapproachable. After her father's death "a few of the ladies had the *temerity* to call"; when she offends them with the smell, the town complains not to her but to the judge, and "in *diffident* deprecation." When they do act, it is secretly and guiltily: "So the next night, after midnight, four men crossed Miss Emily's lawn and *slunk about the house like burglars. . . .*" The men who actually succeeded in seeing her are either ordered out imperiously (the tax-collecting Aldermen) or are treated in some unmentionable way. For instance, the Baptist minister—"The men did not want to interfere, but at the last the ladies forced the Baptist minister . . . to call upon her. He would never divulge what happened during that interview, but he refused to go back again." So with the druggist who sells her arsenic though she refuses to meet the law and tell him why she wants it—"Miss Emily just stared at him . . . the druggist didn't come back." Still, they take care of her almost worshipfully: "Alive, Miss Emily had been a tradition, a duty, and a care; a sort of hereditary obligation upon the town. . . ." She is rather like a goddess in her temple, cool and unapproachable and vaguely frightening,[22] and like so many terrible mythical goddesses, she chooses a man of lower station, has an affair with him, and then kills him to gratify her own needs.

To see someone as godlike is to see that person the way a child sees a parent; in the case of Miss Emily, a particularly distant, unapproachable, and frightening parent.

The infantile curiosity of the narrator spies upon the parent, needing to know from minute to minute where she is and what she is doing. He is curious about her sexuality and he will eventually decide that she is degraded, but for a while he seems to need to believe she is virginal. He says she looks "like a girl," like "those angels in colored church windows," and in tableau with her father, "a slender figure in white." The virginal mother-figure is ironically kept so by her father[23] for in that tableau the town sees Miss Emily "in the background, her father a spraddled silhouette in the foreground, his back to her and clutching a horsewhip. . . ." They remember "all the young men her father had driven away" so that "when she got to be thirty . . . [she] was still single." "None of the young men were quite good enough for Miss Emily and such." A father who allows no man near his daughter is keeping her viginity intact.

Colonel Sartoris and Judge Stevens perform much the same function as Grierson does, for they both protect Miss Emily from being or seeming anything but pure, free of human grossness. Colonel Sartoris exempts her from paying taxes to the town, eighty-year-old Judge Stevens refuses to believe that the smell can be anything but a rat killed by Miss Emily's servant. In effect these men say: money is dirty—a lady should have nothing to do with it; and smell is dirty—a lady can in no way be responsible for it; men (the suitors) and sex are dirty—a lady must be protected from such.

Even after Emily begins to see Homer Barron and when it becomes clear to everyone that she has fallen, the narrator seems to wish to believe she can be restored if not to virginity, at least to chastity. He stresses that she somehow kept "her dignity," and that everyone believed "'She will marry him. . . . She will persuade him yet.'" When the town saw her buying toilet articles and men's clothes, "we said, 'They are married.' We were really glad. We were glad because the two female cousins were even more Grierson than Miss Emily had ever been," and "we were all Miss Emily's allies to help circumvent the cousins," who, we assume, wished her not to marry Homer Barron.

And when this effort fails, the narrator goes a step further. He masculinizes Miss Emily. Twice he calls her "impervious" (impenetrable) as if to stress that she is not even anatomically equipped so that a man could have sexual relations with her, as if she were, in fact, woman-with-a-phallus (the mother known by the child before he finds out that human beings come in two sexes). The first step in her masculinization occurs just before she meets Homer Barron, as if in defensive anticipation of her downfall and beforehand denial that it can happen: she is described as having had "her hair . . . cut short . . . ," boyishly. Then she is identified with her father in her unusual strength of will, and finally her hair is again described in masculine terms: "Up to the day of her death at seventy-four it was still that vigorous iron-gray, like the hair of an active man." The narrator seems to have regressed to a very early stage of maternal relations in order to defend against having to see her as anything but virginal.

The virginal Miss Emily does not remain so, however, for apparently she herself does not wish it. She chooses for a mate a day-laborer and a Yankee who, unlike those aristocrats Sartoris, Stevens, and Grierson, is no respecter of Southern womanhood. Furthermore, "Homer himself had remarked—he liked men, and it was known that he drank with the younger men in the Elks' Club—that he was not a marrying man." Father-attached as she is, she can only choose a man who will disgrace and abandon her. So she kills him out of rage and disappointment and keeps the body out of love and need to deny her loss.

But what does Homer Barron mean to the narrator? He means, first, disillusionment with Emily, kept unapproachable hence pure by the powerful, horsewhip-wielding father, now degraded into an object of gossip behind silken fans and into a woman from whom (via the symbolism of her house as her body) a disgusting odor will emanate (the rotting corpse). Miss Emily was the mother as virgin; now she is the mother as whore. But if she is a source of disillusionment, it is because the voyeurism of the narrator has had some success in wresting from her her secrets. Now she also becomes source of the most intense curiosity the narrator displays anywhere in the story (with the possible exception of the climax). Kempton counted forty-eight "we's" in "A Rose for Emily"; [24] twenty-five of those appear all densely packed together in the few pages that describe the Homer Barron courtship.

We might expect Homer to become oedipal rival to the narrator, too, for the voyeurism of the child-consciousness directs itself to discovering what the mysterious relationship between adult men and women means and to trying at some time to replace one of his parents in the affections and bed of the other. Perhaps the aggression and sadism the narrator directs against Miss Emily are caused in part by the fact that she should engage so flagrantly in a love relationship with the man rather than with the narrator. To him, Homer Barron must be a potent but worthless male: "Homer Barron, a Yankee—a big, dark, ready man, with a big voice. . . ." "Homer Barron with his hat cocked and a cigar in his teeth. . . ." And the ladies are sure that "'a Grierson would not think seriously of a Northerner, a day laborer.'"

But despite these obvious oedipal elements, we must go slowly on affirming that Homer Barron is oedipal rival to the narrator. In a fully developed and "normal" oedipal stage, we would expect at least a clear sexual differentiation among the participants; say, son (male), mother (female), father (male). Only after this is established, only after the child has reached the phallic stage, when the boy appreciates the value and pleasure of as well as the possible dangers to this phallus; when he recognizes that it has something or other to do with the sexual relationship between his parents; when he wishes to become his own mother's spouse and oust that loved-and-hated rival, his father; and when, finally, he must for the sake of keeping his phallus give up his mother—only when we have at least the rudimentary pattern of this can we say we have an oedipal conflict. But in "A Rose for Emily" the sexual demarcation of participants is not clear. Emily is a woman, Homer Barron is a man, but what is the narrator? Faulkner seems to have invested considerable creative effort in keeping that narrator not only sexless but plural. Because of the blurred sexuality of the most significant participant in the oedipal situation, we must say that while "A Rose for Emily" does begin to sketch in oedipal conflicts among narrator and Homer Barron and Emily, the most powerful unconscious currents of the story move in pre-oedipal depths. Even the phallic intrusion of the narrator into Miss Emily's privacy is expressed regressively, through the eyes. Voyeurism, aggression, and sadism directed at Miss Emily—these are the powerful pre-oedipal conflicts animating the story.

VII

But another and even more primitive psychological conflict animates "A Rose for Emily." It is anxiety over loss of the loved object. From Emily's point of view, the story concerns a woman's inability or unwillingness to sustain the loss of the loved man (father, protector, or lover). From the narrator's point of view, the story is also concerned with anxieties over loss, though his object, Miss Emily, lives a long time. His voyeurism, sadism, and aggression are all bound up with his loss fears (as well as with his quest for sexual information and stimulation). For instance, the voyeurism is sexualized looking, exercised by the narrator both erotically and aggressively as a phallic intrusion, but it is also a kind of eating-up-with-the-eyes used to ensure that the needed object does not abandon her dependants. The sixty-year scrutiny of the narrator seems to be saying, "I watch her so intently and so long to assure myself that she is still there. I take her into myself through my eyes so that, being inside me, I can control her[25] and prevent her from going away. Further, I tell this story about her and so manage to keep her with me even after she is dead. She kept the dead Homer Barron in her room because she would not accept his loss; I keep the dead Miss Emily, too, but in the form of a story."

The narrator expresses his loss anxiety most clearly in his constant watching of Miss Emily and reporting what he sees; he also expresses that anxiety by his reporting on times he does *not* see that eccentric recluse. Miss Emily "no longer went out at all;" the Board of Aldermen "knocked at the door through which no visitor had passed since she ceased giving china-painting lessons eight or ten years earlier;" "after her father's death she went out very little; after her sweetheart went away, people hardly saw her at all;" "and that was the last we saw of Homer Barron. And of Miss Emily for some time . . . for almost six months she did not appear on the streets;" "from that time on her front door remained closed." In fact for all the sixty years of the narrator's looking, he can have seen her very little.

He expresses loss anxiety, too, in a concern about whether Miss Emily sees him or not in concern about how Miss Emily uses her eyes. "Now and then we would see her in one of the downstairs windows—she had evidently shut up the top floor of the house—like the carven torso of an idol in a niche, *looking or not looking at us,* we could never tell which." When Miss Emily ever does look at anyone, it is sightlessly, coldly: "Her eyes, lost in the fatty ridges of her face, looked like two small pieces of coal pressed into a lump of dough as they moved from one face to another. . . ." She had "cold, haughty black eyes. . . ." Worse, Miss Emily is capable of aggressive, even destructive looking such as she does when she stares down the druggist, so compelling him to sell her poison: "Miss Emily just stared at him, her head tilted back in order to look him eye for eye, until he looked away and went and got the arsenic and wrapped it up. The Negro delivery boy brought her the package; the druggist didn't come back."

Seeing the loved person is reassurance against loss; being seen by her can be assurance of love if the regard is warm; but if it is cold and aggressive it must cause anxiety about both being harmed and being left. If the loved person also withdraws from sight, that anxiety must increase even further and must cause rage over frustrated needs. If we add to these the impotence of the watcher to force the needed object to stay near and to be giving, then we can even better understand why Miss Emily should become source of loss anxiety and aggressive attack by the narrator. We can see, too, why he should call her (house) an "eyesore among eyesores"—a description that shows both his aggression ("her house [she] is so ugly it [she] makes my eyes sore") and his need ("I look at her [house] so hard and long that my eyes are sore").

The voyeurism, then, is manifestation of loss anxiety, effort to control the loved object, and aggression against it because of frustration. Now in these latter two functions (to control, to retaliate) the voyeurism becomes cannibalistic. The narrator eats up Miss Emily with his eyes. The text gives abundant support for this assertion, for Faulkner consistently ties eye imagery with food or eating imagery. Miss Emily's aggressive *staring down* of the druggist is performed when she buys *arsenic;* her sitting like an idol in a niche, *looking or not looking* at the men, is performed when those men are

cleansing her house and yard of the smell which they believe is caused by a
dead rat (rotting flesh); Miss Emily's *black eyes* look like coals pressed in
dough, and she is here described as "a small, *fat* woman . . . what would have
been merely *plumpness* in another was *obesity* in her. She looked *bloated.* . . ."
In all these instances, the eye-eating images have to do with killing. One
final eating image seems to support this: "And that was the last we *saw* of
Homer Barron. And of Miss Emily for some time. The Negro man went in
and out with the *market basket.* . . ." "When we next *saw* Miss Emily, she
had *grown fat* and her hair was turning gray."

By associating Miss Emily's aggressive looking with food, fatness, poison, and dead bodies, the narrator seems to be saying that Miss Emily is a
kind of black widow spider or Evil Eye; she kills and then eats her victims.
But of course the reader likely does not take the narrator's grisly hints as
objective truths.[26] More likely they are reflections of the narrator's own
mental construction: for him Miss Emily is poisoner and cannibal. One
might wonder why and one might also ask how Miss Emily's hinted cannibalism proves that the narrator's voyeurism is cannibalistic, too.

Seeing Miss Emily as possessor of the Evil Eye, as poisoner, and as
cannibal are all ways by which the narrator condemns her for being a bad
mother. She should be looking tenderly and assuringly, but she instead hurts
with her gaze; she should nourish, but instead she poisons; she should be
willing to give her own body—milk and breast—for the ones she loves, but
instead she eats the body of her beloved. Seeing her in these ways performs
yet another function. To see mother as cannibal and capable of aggressive
looking is also likely to be a projection of the dependent's own destructive
wishes. He wants to poison and eat her and to kill her with his gaze because
she has sorely frustrated him. And for these wishes he fears talion punishment: "she will eat me, she will kill me with her eyes." The psychological
procedure seems to follow this pattern:

> I love her and do not want to lose her.
> I hate her because she denied me (her presence, her secrets) and betrayed
> me (loved Homer Barron).
>
> I do not want to lose her, so I will eat her up and so keep her inside me
> (eat with the eyes in the constant watching; retain in the body by making up a
> story about her).
> I hate her because of her denial and betrayal, so I will eat her up to pun-
> ish her.

But to eat in love is to lose by death; to want to eat in hate is to be eaten in retaliation.

No, I do not hate her; it is she who hates me and wants to eat me.
No, that is not right either; she does not want to eat me; she wants to eat him (Homer Barron).

Thus the narrator is the would-be-poisoner, cannibal, and Evil Eye, but he projects his aberrations onto Miss Emily because to acknowledge them as his own necessarily intensifies and might even actualize the thing he most fears, that Miss Emily will abandon him.

VIII

Perhaps now we can formulate another level of meaning for "A Rose for Emily" so as to include both its major characters, the watcher and the watched. It is a story about types of perversion—Miss Emily's necrophilia and the narrator's voyeurism that are motivated by frustrated sexual needs and by fears about loss of the loved object. Miss Emily fears and reacts insanely to the loss of loved men—father Grierson, protector Sartoris, and lover Barron; the narrator fears loss of a needed woman, Miss Emily herself, and reacts not psychotically but childishly in his mental aggression, sadism, and voyeurism.

The narrator is a kind of child, at least in his mental patterns. This in part explains the uncanny effect of the story, for by means of the archaic consciousness with which the reader merges, Faulkner stirs depths of discomfort (even horror) appropriate to the kind of story he is telling, creating rich and complex emotional responses that we might know are occurring but that we cannot fully understand. We lapse the more readily into this merger with the narrator because Faulkner has made him both invisible and apparently objective; we therefore assume that only Miss Emily, the object of the narrator's attention, is significant and that the portrait we are given of her is "true" or "accurate." But when we step back from the story and break the fusion we have been drawn into, then certain facts must become clear: that Miss Emily is strained through the perceptions not alone of the author but of a fictional character he has created. Therefore, to determine anything at all about Miss Emily, we must first come to terms with the medium of consciousness through whom she is perceived. Miss Emily is the Miss Emily the narrator sees.

NOTES

[1]   Kenneth Payson Kempton, *The Short Story* (Cambridge : Harvard University Press, 1948), p. 104.

[2]   For convenience, the narrator-group will from now on be referred to as "he."

[3]   Austin McGiffert Wright, *The American Short Story in the Twenties* (Chicago: University of Chicago Press, 1961), p. 334.

[4]   Cleanth Brooks and Robert Penn Warren, *Understanding Fiction*, 2nd ed. (New York: Appleton-Century-Crofts, 1959), p. 352.

[5]   *Ibid.*, p. 353.

[6]   For instance, they seem not to be older because they refer to the Confederate veterans who attend her funeral (she is seventy-four, they must be about ninety) as "them" and as the "very old men." The narrator seems not to be younger for he refers to "the rising generation" as "they," too: "they mailed her a tax notice," "they called a special meeting of the Board of Aldermen." But he seems not to be of her exact generation, either, for he speaks as though that generation were different from his own. When Colonel Sartoris concocts the tale to justify the town's remitting of Miss Emily's taxes, the narrator comments, "Only a man of Colonel Sartoris' generation and thought could have invented it, and only a woman could have believed it." (All quotations from "A Rose for Emily" come from *Collected Stories of William Faulkner* [New York: Random House, 1950].)

[7]   Henceforth all emphases in quotations from "A Rose for Emily" and critical articles are mine.

[8]   The town's ambivalence toward Emily seems to be a reflection of Faulkner's own ambivalence toward the South. "Faulkner, in all his works, shows . . . an ambivalence toward the South. And in none of his works, it seems to me, is the paradox so neatly compressed as in Emily. The whole texture of the story is wrought of this ambivalence of love and hate, respect and contempt." Sister Mary Bride, "Faulkner's *A Rose for Emily*," *Explicator*, 20 (May 1962), Item 78.

[9]   Floyd C. Watkins, "The Structure of 'A Rose for Emily,'" *Modern Language Notes*, 69 (November 1954), 509.

[10]   *Ibid.*

[11]   Elmo Howell, "Faulkner's *A Rose for Emily*," *Explicator*, 19 (January 1961), Item 26.

[12]   John V. Hagopian, "Faulkner's *A Rose for Emily*," *Explicator*, 22 (April 1964), Item 68.

[13]   For further discussion see Arthur C. Clements, "Faulkner's *A Rose for Emily*," *Explicator*, 20 (May 1962), Item 78; and George Snell, *The Shapers of American Fiction, 1798 1947* (New York: Cooper Square, 1947), p. 98.

[14]   Norman N. Holland in an unpublished paper, "Phases, Fictions, and Nations: 'A Rose for Emily' and a Task for the Developmental Model," also sees the climax as primal scene fantasy, a fantasy defended against by being far removed in time. "Time is clearly one of the defensive modes the story uses, for it gives us, not the bridal night, but the bridal night

forty years later, utterly still, silent, finished. In effect, any frightening noise or sight or movement is denied" (p. 24). Dr. Holland's valuable paper, which analyzes Emily Grierson herself, was the stimulus for this paper.

15 A child does not usually know that womb and bowels are different, hence it can fantasy that babies come from the bowels and are made of feces (that feces are baby). And sometimes when he speculates about where mother's penis is, he believes that the fecal column is the penis and that it lies temporarily inside the body.

16 Ray B. West, Jr., "Atmosphere and Theme in Faulkner's 'A Rose for Emily,'" in *William Faulkner: Two Decades of Criticism*, ed. by Frederick J. Hoffman and Olga W. Vickery (East Lansing: Michigan State College Press, 1951), p. 260.

17 *Ibid.*, p. 265.

18 *Ibid.*

19 Bride, Item 78.

20 Wright, p. 322.

21 For further discussions see William T. Going, "Chronology in Teaching 'A Rose for Emily,'" *Exercise Exchange*, 5 (February 1958), 8–11; Paul D. McGlynn, "The Chronology of 'A Rose for Emily,'" *Studies in Short Fiction*, 6 (Summer 1969), 461–62; and Robert W. Woodward, "The Chronology of 'A Rose for Emily,'" *Exercise Exchange*, 13 (March 1966), 17–19.

22 Faulkner himself said of Miss Emily, "I feel sorry for Emily's tragedy. . . . I pity Emily. I don't know whether I would have liked her or not, I might have been afraid of her." *Lion in the Garden: Interviews with William Faulkner, 1926–1962*, ed. by James B. Meriwether and Michael Millgate (New York: Random House, 1968), p. 127.

23 Norman Holland in the paper previously referred to speaks of the relationship between Emily and her father in oedipal terms, a view supported by Faulkner himself: "There was a young girl with a young girl's normal aspirations to find love and then a husband and a family, who was brow-beaten and kept down by her father, a selfish man. . . ." *Faulkner in the University*, ed. by Frederick L. Gwynn and Joseph L. Blotner (Charlottesville: University of Virginia Press, 1959), p. 185.
Irving Malin speaks of the oedipal relationship, too: "Her passionate, almost sexual relationship with her dead father forces her to distrust the living body of Homer and to kill him so that he will resemble the dead father she can never forget." *William Faulkner: An Interpretation* (Stanford: Stanford University Press, 1957), p. 37.
My analysis shifts focus on the father because whatever he might mean if we look at Emily's story from her perspective, he means something else when the story is viewed from the narrator's. Then the oedipal rival would not be Emily's father but her lover, Homer Barron.

24 Kempton, p. 106.

25 Norman sees need for control as important in this story. "Certainly control is a basic issue of the story, not only for Miss Emily, but also in the town from whose point of view we see her. Repeatedly, we hear about the forces of law in the town. . . ." (pp. 14–15). He points out how often (and how ineffectually) the town tries to control her through various

legal means. Such methods for achieving control point to anal issues, issues which I, too, see as significant in the story. And beneath the anxieties about loss in the anal stage lie loss anxieties in the oral stage. In fact we can see fear of loss in all three stages, oral, anal, phallic (oedipal) in the narrator's consciousness as well as in Miss Emily's.

²⁶ What "really" happened and what is narrator's opinion and feeling about events is, of course, a major issue in such a story as "A Rose for Emily." I am assuming here and everywhere in this essay that events are facts but any comment and most description of those events are not facts but reflections of the narrator's psychology. Thus, the father driving away suitors, Miss Emily buying arsenic, and the finding of a skeleton on the bed are facts, but all remarks on these events (like, "that quality of her father which had thwarted her woman's life so many times") or sinister suggestions arising from juxtaposition of event with event (like how after Homer Barron disappeared Miss Emily grew fat) are part of the narrator's psychology.

ISAAC RODMAN

Irony and Isolation: Narrative Distance in Faulkner's "A Rose for Emily"

The critical consensus remains that the narrator of "A Rose for Emily" speaks for his community.[1] The narrator has been seen as "community representative" (Allen 187); "[t]he narrating character in 'A Rose for Emily' plays no active role, but his opinions of Emily Grierson directly reflect his community's attitude" (Ruppersburg 15). For another critic, "the first person narrator . . . seems to represent the generalized voice of Jefferson" (Millgate, *Achievement* 272). Cleanth Brooks wrote:

> In "A Rose for Emily" . . . there is a narrator who . . . clearly speaks for the community. For example, he never says "I thought," or "I knew," or "I believed," but speaks rather of "our whole town"; he says that "we were not pleased" at certain happenings. . . . This anonymous speaker never insists on his individual judgments. (The community is a true community and he is clearly its voice.) (158)[2]

But the narrator may be seen to be as isolated as Miss Emily herself, or as Faulkner himself as a young man. Emily Grierson's predicament reflects the narrator's also as he tells his story.

The narrator is more dedicated to ironic distance than to identification with the people of the town. He keeps the town's secret while giving it away—keeps it on the literal level, as the town does, and gives it away on the level of figure, allusion, and association. He implies "*We* did not see," but he presents what was there to be seen. And on a deeper level he implies in his diction that he stands apart from the limited perception of the town.

The narrative weave contains two voices, that of a surface narrator who accurately portrays the voice of the town, and that of a deeper narrator who conceals his judgments but allows his tone to indicate his perspective to literarily inclined readers. The deeper narrative implies Faulknerian isolation on the part of the very narrator who speaks as the voice of the town.

Early in the story the narrator establishes himself as the kind of person who catches a reader's attention with his self-conscious images.[3] We accept him as a story-teller: the daring yet comfortably cute paradox of the early descriptions of Emily Grierson's house as "heavily lightsome" and rising with "stubborn and coquettish decay" establishes the narrator as one who sees associations beyond the imaginative ken of the ordinary townspeople, and the solipsism of "cedar-bemused cemetery" elevates the narrator above the town on his own petard of ironic distance.

Even in the first sentence the narrator's image-making gives the reader an experience of the way the town casts Emily in a lifeless mold. She is a "fallen monument." Monuments are inanimate representations of past glory, and at least since Hemingway in *A Farewell to Arms* reflected a modernist suspicion of grand adjectives and acceptance only of the names of places where people have acted with dignity,[4] traditional monuments are especially lifeless to the modern sensibility. (The monolith of the Vietnam War Memorial in Washington embodies this rejection of the traditional aesthetic.) As early as the first sentence of "A Rose for Emily," the narrator establishes both the traditional connotation of monument and the seeds of its rejection.

In the first sentence our readerly defenses are lulled by the "respectful affection" the men feel for the fallen monument. The rhetorical focus is on the "respectful affection" and not on the connotations of "monument" as applied to a human being. The word *monument* is slipped in as the object of a preposition, in a phrase, that is, that carries its own diminution of importance, its own "low profile" as an appendage to the rhetorical centers of the sentence (subject, verb, object). On a first reading, the fact that the women of the town go to Emily's funeral "mostly out of curiosity to see the inside of her house" is elided in humor. The town's rhetorical strategy is to lull auditors into an acceptance that is, on the second level, unacceptable to the deeper narrative, and to the author standing behind the narrator's limitations. It is a natural impulse to want to see inside a house that has been closed to visitors for ten years—but for the narrator to present this as the only reason mentioned that the women of the town attend the funeral is telling about a lack of sympathy. So in the first paragraph, the narrator has shown himself by his selection of details (the women's reason to visit the house) and by the witty detachment of his images (fallen monument, stubborn and coquettish decay, cedar-bemused cemetery) to hold himself at a certain ironic distance from his fellow townspeople.

Evidence of this narrator's irony may be traced throughout the story. By the time "we" say "'Poor Emily'" behind the jalousies as they [Emily Grierson and Homer Barron] passed on Sunday afternoon in the glittering buggy," the narrator, rather than being there among those calling Emily lost, comments on the commenters. If he was there and maybe even said it, he said it with a sense of his saying it because it was the thing to say, a sense of his playing his role in the theater of the town. As far as the town is concerned, he is still one of "us." The town is his, but, like Emily, he is isolated from true belonging in a loneliness of narrative distance that makes the subject of his story not only the subject in a narrative sense (Emily), but also the subject in the psychological sense (the narrator himself).

Emily, her woman's life thwarted, is left to exist as the last of an aristocratic line, as an eccentric recluse, or as an idol, a fallen monument, showing its gilded crown but also its feet of clay. (The narrator cites the wisdom of the town: "People in our town, remembering how old lady Wyatt, her great-aunt, had gone completely crazy at last, believed that the Griersons held themselves a little too high for what they really were." The narrator too exists in a rarified linguistic stratum, talking to the town but above it, isolating himself by his superior rhetoric as Faulkner isolated himself from the other students in Oxford, Mississippi (Blotner 264).

Faulkner was called "Count No-Count" by his fellow students at Ole Miss. But the irony of this situation is that, as can be seen in the details Blotner supplies, Faulkner had no fellow students in Oxford—in the sense of students with whom he shared fellowship. Blotner quotes an observer: "It was partly Faulkner's fault. . . . he had rather needlessly offended many of the students by what they thought his 'arrogance'; the way he was believed to 'put on airs'" (264). "During that period of his life Faulkner was almost painfully shy; he felt that many of the other students did not like him, and he retaliated by affecting a total indifference he did not totally feel" (254). But the Francophile poetry Faulkner published while in Oxford (not to mention the skilled Beardsley-esque drawings) was competent and poignant (if perhaps derivative), while the lampoons of Faulkner published by the other students were not even grammatical (see Blotner 264). Faulkner, who had not yet adopted his protective pose of a farmer who just happened to write, was isolated in his linguistic competence. At this time he was consciously a war hero (a fabrication) and a writer (real enough even then, but not a pose designed to win acceptance among the other literary poseurs at the university). Like the Griersons, Faulkner held himself "a little too high" for the tastes of his neighbors, and there was some truth in the perceptions of both towns, Emily's and Faulkner's.

The town is unable to think of Emily as a human being with needs. This limitation of perception is implied in the narrator's presentation of the town's thinking of her as an idol. But beyond that, consider the time "we" all said "'She will kill herself'; and we said it would be the best thing." At this point the reader has either been drawn into the town's view and has accepted the Lucretian code of Southern chivalry that could lead to such a statement, and therefore accepts the narrator's "we" at face value, or the reader has realized that the narrator and the reader are involved in the irony of a subtle collusion against the town that mirrors the town's subtle collusion against Emily.

It is of course possible at this point that the narrator loves his town with a faint bemused detachment, much as the town "loves" Emily when it finds her "a tradition, a duty, and a care; a sort of hereditary obligation," but the retrospective quality of the narration, recalled some time after the finding of the hair, casts doubt on this possibility. To see the narrator as representative of the consciousness of the town would be an overgenerous perception of the town's ability to objectify itself.

A major problem in the story is the seeming inability of the townspeople to associate the smell of decaying meat with the disappearance of Homer Barron. Although the point is never made explicitly in the story, this inability seems willed, at least on an unconscious level. As surely as a gentleman does not tell a lady she smells ("'Dammit, sir,' Judge Stevens said, 'will you accuse a lady to her face of smelling bad?'"), a closed Southern town does not send its venerable idol to jail or asylum for murdering a Yankee.

Section II of the story, about the smell (and about the death of Emily's father), demonstrates the willful blindness of the townspeople. Although they recognize the smell as that of a dead and decaying animal ("It's probably just a snake or a rat . . . killed in the yard"), they do not reexamine their assumption that "her sweetheart . . . had deserted her" in the light of the evidence of animal decay. They do not allow these separate data to mix in the collective mind.

This isolation of data is especially curious because in Section IV we learn that the town knew that Homer Barron had returned before the smell (although his return is not allowed to be associated with the smell): "Within three days Homer Barron was back in town. A neighbor saw . . . him at the kitchen door at dusk one evening." And no one ever saw him leave again. A reasonable assumption is that, in this town, if he had left, someone would have seen him somewhere between Emily's house and the train station, and "we" all would have heard about it. The seeming inability to reflect on causality where one of their own is concerned characterizes a perversely limited perception expressed by the contorted chronology of the narration.

Much futile ink has been spilled over chronology in "Emily." Brooks (386) observes that "At least six chronologies of this story have been produced. Miss Emily's death is variously set at 1924, 1928, 1934, 1937." Despite the discrepancies among chronologies various readers had constructed, Brooks still forged ahead to try his own—somewhat of a compromise. He fell into the same trap the others had. Chronologies fail if they try to identify specific dates of events. This specificity is impossible because of the vagueness and confusion of reference in the text, and that vagueness reflects the epistemology of the townspeople. Also, considering the ages of the Civil War veterans at the funeral, any chronology must be suspected of being a little more mythic than realistic. Dates are not important. They are external to the story, which does not exist in any known system of years beyond its own. What is relevant to the story is its internal time scheme or, rather, lack of it—the way parts relate, or fail to relate, within the story. This lack of chronological relationship is relevant because it is central to the problems of the story—personal relationships, perceptions, epistemology: how the townspeople know what they know, and how they insulate themselves from other knowledge. The confused time sequence of the story may be seen to represent the way the townspeople compartmentalize their thoughts— insulating dangerous reagents from hazardous interaction. The narrator's irony results in part from his telling of the story after the discovery of the hair in language that reflects the town's consciousness before the discovery. Consider for instance this paragraph:

> And that was the last we saw of Homer Barron. And of Miss Emily for some time. The . . . front door remained closed. Now and then we would see her at a window for a moment, as the men did that night when they sprinkled the lime, but for almost six months she did not appear on the streets. Then we knew that this was to be expected too; as if that quality of her father which had thwarted her woman's life had been too virulent and too furious to die.

The narrator seems to claim that Emily locks herself up after her lover leaves (as the town professes to believe, although a rereading shows that they believed this about the time the smell started and that they knew the nature of the smell) because of her father's thwarting her life and because of the patterns of behavior she learned under his control. But the paragraph works better during a rereading, when the reader is aware of the body in the bed upstairs—but works better only if we imagine the town has made the same connection—in other words, has at some level connected the smell with the disappearance of the lover, even if this connection was never admitted consciously. Here Homer Barron's disappearance, Emily's becoming a recluse, the smell, and her father's furious thwarting of her normal sexual development are all juxtaposed in one paragraph. Proximity would seem to demand association, but the town's mind is protected from such association with the dark side of its psyche as it was from association with the darker-skinned people of the region. The smell is conceived in a simile, which can be dropped from a syntactical construction without altering the meaning of the remainder. Thus language mirrors the epistemology of the town: because the categories of perception are different, phenomena in chronological proximity are not together in thought if they are classified, grouped, and processed differently, at least in conscious thought. On a deeper level, these connections are probably made, but the collective conscious mind rejects them in defense of Emily as "one of us" on that level, although resented as haughty on another level. Like Emily and the narrator as persons, data are isolated as abstractions as the town processes some information and refuses to process other.

Not only are groupings in the town's narrative associational, but the chronology that does exist is vague, couched in expressions like "a period of six or seven years, when she was about forty." This vagueness seems to serve the willful blindness of the townspeople by creating a confusion that allows them to ignore, for instance, the proximity among the purchase of the arsenic, the disappearance of Homer Barron, and the smell. As a matter of fact, if the vague time references are forced into a linear chronology, it seems that the narrator claims that the arsenic was purchased after the other two events, although of course this claim is very indirect and made while juggling several other narrative events and making believe that there is no connection at all and therefore there is no claim to make. This implied claim is possible (or rather the evidence can be arranged to give this impression) because the issue is never addressed. The chronologies of the different events are given in different sequences, different episodes. The town assumes that a spinster would purchase arsenic to kill herself. The thought that she would poison a Yankee suitor does not even form to be denied. To a reader's hindsight, this compartmentalization of events takes on the quality of dramatic irony (the perception or knowledge of the audience being superior to that of the characters).

The townspeople's perceptions do not threaten their preconceptions. Emily is at once a winner and a loser to this form of perception, this selective blindness. She wins in that she gets away with murder because the town thinks of her as an idol and not as a murderess. But she is a loser because of the same idolization. The town is content to regard her as its petted eccentric rather than as a frustrated human being. The town shared "that quality of her father which had thwarted her woman's life so many times."

For all their spite about Homer Barron's qualifications to court Emily, the town seems genuinely happy for her when it seems that she will marry him. ("We said, 'They are married.' We were really glad. . . . By that time it was a cabal, and we were all Miss Emily's allies . . .") "They are married" is a curious statement for the town, another example of selective blindness. Can we doubt that if Emily had stood in front of any preacher or judge and said *I do,* within a few hours everyone in this town would have known exactly when and where the event took place and what the bride wore, and probably too what scandalously inappropriate clothes Homer Barron wore, even if there had been an elopement and secret ceremony in another town? At this point the willful blindness of the town extends even to extenuating what was previously seen as Emily's ruination.

And what has intervened? The purchase of the arsenic, to which the town's response was "She will kill herself" and "It would be the best thing." Without a qualm or a tear, the town is willing to dedicate Emily on the altar of Southern gentility, making of their idol a blood sacrifice. Emily at this point has no meaning for the town except as a Form of form. Nothing is made of this sequence:

> purchase of rat poison
> "she will kill herself," "it would be the best thing"
> "'We were sure they were to be married.' . . . We were really glad."

This sequence is made the straight line for a joke. The punch line, immediately following, is "We were glad because the two female cousins were even more Grierson than Miss Emily had ever been" (so the town was glad they would take their haughty ways back to Alabama). The sequence is given secondary rhetorical weight by being made a straight line; the reader's attention is thus diverted again, as the town diverted its own attention with front-porch philosophizing and wise-cracking. Entertainment values override human sympathy: "We sat back to watch developments," the narrator reports. In retrospect, with the last paragraph in mind, this sentence comments on the town more than on the objects of its attention.

The sequence is not only not insisted upon, it is obscured in the shifts of time, the fancy shuffles of the chronological deck in the croupier narrator's hands. It is as if the town experiences contrition for wishing Emily dead, and in repentance is willing to accept the Yankee loudmouth as her husband. At this point the town remembers seeing Homer Barron return at dusk to the kitchen door—a fact never correlated to the arsenic or the smell.

Although they do not accept Homer Barron as a suitor, the towns-people profess to be "really glad" when they believe Emily has married him. Is this merely graceful acceptance of a *fait accompli*? The townspeople know that "the quality of her father which had thwarted her woman's life so many times had been too virulent and too furious to die," and this knowing entails compassion, a "feeling with."

The town is more chorus than agent. This story can be seen as the town's tragedy. The town witnesses, and is powerless to prevent, the decay of one of its leading citizens, one of its idols. The narrator may be the only member of the community to examine his perceptions of Emily's isolation and to supply them in a narrative that renders the data available to reinterpretation on a re-reading, but the narrator chooses the conceptual doubling of dramatic irony rather than a break with his community. The narrator, while part of the town and speaking for the town, has distanced himself from the town and retains for himself the sanity and the loneliness of the literary perspective.

WORKS CITED

Allen, Dennis W. "Horror and Perverse Delight: Faulkner's 'A Rose for Emily.'" *Modern Fiction Studies* 30 (1984): 685–96.

Allen, Walter. *The Short Story in English*. New York: Oxford UP, 1981.

Beck, Warren. *Faulkner: Essays*. Madison: U of Wisconsin P, 1976.

Blotner, Joseph L. *William Faulkner: A Biography*. 2 vols. New York: Random House, 1974.

Brooks, Cleanth. *William Faulkner: The Yoknapatawpha Country*. New Haven: Yale UP, 1963.

———. *William Faulkner: Toward Yoknapatawpha and Beyond*. New Haven: Yale UP, 1978.

Everett, Walter K. *Faulkner's Art and Characters*. New York: Barron's, 1969.

Faulkner, William. *Collected Stories of William Faulkner*. New York: Random House, 1950.

Hays, Peter L. "Who Is Faulkner's Emily?" *Studies in American Fiction* 16 (1988): 105–10.

Hemingway, Ernest. *A Farewell to Arms*. New York: Scribner's, 1929.

Jacobs, John T. "Ironic Allusions in 'A Rose for Emily.'" *Notes on Mississippi Writers* 14 (1982): 77–79.

Kurtz, Elizabeth Carney. "Faulkner's 'A Rose for Emily.'" *Explicator* 44 (1986): 40.

Littler, Frank A. "The Tangled Thread of Time: Faulkner's 'A Rose for Emily.'" *Notes on Mississippi Writers* XIV (1982): 80–86.

Millgate, Michael. "William Faulkner: The Problem of Point of View." *William Faulkner: Four Decades of Criticism*. Ed. Linda Welshimer Wagner. East Lansing: Michigan State UP, 1973. 179–91.

———. *The Achievement of William Faulkner* (1966). Lincoln: U of Nebraska P, 1978.

Petry, Alice Hall. "Faulkner's 'A Rose for Emily.'" *Explicator* 44 (1986): 52–54.

Porter, Carolyn. *Seeing and Being: The Plight of the Participant Observer in Emerson, James, Adams, and Faulkner*. Middletown: Wesleyan UP, 1981.

Reed, Joseph W., Jr. *Faulkner's Narrative*. New Haven and London: Yale UP, 1973.

Ruppersburg, Hugh M. *Voice and Eye in Faulkner's Fiction*. Athens: U of Georgia P, 1983.

NOTES

[1] Several recent works with promising titles either do not address the issue of this paper or ignore discussions of "A Rose for Emily." See, for example, Dennis Allen (whose subject is sexuality and death); Beck (who considers Faulkner's world view and concludes that Faulkner is not a nihilist and that his characters are not he); Hays (who considers historical models for the character of Emily); Jacobs; Kurtz (who considers the rose as a symbol of loneliness and frustration); Littler (whose subject is chronology); Millgate ([1973] whose subject is interior monologues in the novels; his 1966 book does not consider this subject); Petry (who deals with diction); and Porter (who does not include "A Rose for Emily" in her study). Millgate sees "the central theme" to be Emily's "withdrawal into unreality and illusion" (*Achievement* 264). An implication of this paper is that the town's failure in perception may be seen as the central theme, and it forms the point of departure for the narrative consciousness. Everett argues that in the "epiphany" "[t]he reader and the narrator simultaneously recognize the deeper implications of Emily's situation" (165–67), but his discussion does not extend this insight back into a re-examination of the narration itself, which is performed after the "epiphany" and is a result of the narrator's post-lapsarian perspective.

While an interesting paper might be written contending that the narrator is female, such a claim would have to constitute a thesis of its own and could not be included as an obiter dictum here. For the sake of this paper, let us assume that the speaker of "only a woman could believe it" is a man.

[2] Brooks in 1963 had hinted at the line he developed in 1978. "There are plenty of hints in Faulkner's work pointing to the pervasive sense of the community. In 'A Rose for Emily' . . . the narrator writes: 'We had long thought'; 'We did not say she was crazy then'; 'At first we were glad'; etc" (*Yoknapatawpha* 377).

Brooks' later analysis (1978) is more complex. He recognizes that the community is not monolithic; its "subgroupings . . . have their differing emphases" (159), and his declaration that the narrator is clearly a community voice becomes less and less meaningful as his analysis continues. "The narrator is presumably not one of the remaining Civil War veterans," and he is "not a member of the younger generation either, or if he is in actual years, he is far from sympathetic with their ideas and he does not identify himself with them." "Though he is immersed in the customs and beliefs and values of the Jefferson community, he has, nevertheless, a good observer's detachment. He is also an accomplished story-teller." Brooks' analysis occasionally becomes impressionistic: "I think of him as man in his fifties or sixties at the time of Miss Emily's death" (*Toward*, 159), but it is the implications of the "good observer's detachment" that this paper considers.

The narrator's being an accomplished story-teller we may want to attribute more to Faulkner's use of the conventions of storytelling (where narrators are often more articulate than most people) than to insight into the narrator's character, but to make my argument I too depend upon the narrator's use of language. While Brooks recognizes that the community is not monolithic, he never withdraws from his position that the narrator is clearly a community voice.

³ This sentence might tendentiously read, "Faulkner early establishes the narrator as a person. . . ." To say the narrator establishes himself indicates the narrator's layering of voices.

⁴ Hemingway's narrator muses, "I was always embarrassed by the words sacred, glorious, and sacrifice and the expression in vain. We had heard them, sometimes standing in the rain almost out of earshot, so that only the shouted words came through, and had read them, on proclamations that were slapped up by billposters over other proclamations, now for a long time, and I had seen nothing sacred, and the things that were glorious had no glory and the sacrifices were like the stockyards at Chicago if nothing was done with the meat except to bury it. There were many words that you could not stand to hear and finally only the names of places had dignity. . . . Abstract words such as glory, honor, courage, or hallow were obscene beside the concrete names of villages, the numbers of roads, the names of rivers, the numbers of regiments and the dates" (184).

ROBERT CROSMAN

How Readers Make Meaning

For a number or years now I have been arguing that readers make the meanings of literary texts, and that accordingly there is no such thing as "right reading." Such a conclusion troubles most students of literature, and raises a host of questions, some of which—like "By what authority can I tell a student his interpretation is wrong?" or "How then can English be called a discipline?"—are questions of campus politics that are, theoretically at least, very easily answered. The problem for us is to answer the much more complex question of *how* readers make meaning: under what impulses or constraints, following what conventions or strategies? Beyond this lies a second thorny question: are different readers' results all equally valid?¹

I want to try answering these general questions by looking at a specific text—William Faulkner's short story "A Rose for Emily"—and two antithetical interpretations of it. My contention is that although these interpretations contradict each other, both are valid. How this can be, it will be my task to explain. The two readers are myself and one of the students in a course called "Responses to Literature" that I taught at Trinity College in 1976. Our procedure was to read a text, and then immediately to write in our journals about our thoughts, feelings, and fantasies during and after reading. Here first is my journal entry, warts and all, exactly as I wrote it:

This is a story I had never actually read, though I had heard of it, read something about it, and in particular knew its ending, which kept me from feeling the pure shock that the reader must feel who knows nothing of what is coming. Even so I felt a shock, and reacted with an audible cry of mingled loathing and pleasure at the final and most shocking discovery: that Emily has slept with this cadaver for forty years. The loathing is easy enough to explain: the problem is to explain the pleasure. But before trying, let me record other parts of my "response."

I found my mind wandering as I read this story; there were paragraphs I had to reread several times. For one reason or another I was "uninvolved" with the story, perhaps a product of the circumstances under which I read it, but possibly also a response to the story itself. There are various reasons why I might tonight shun wrestling with a "serious" story, but perhaps I also shrank from the "horror" I knew was coming. Perhaps the story of a woman killing her faithless lover is not one I particularly want to hear. I've known about this story for years, yet had no urge to read it, perhaps because I knew what it contained.

She kills him. What do I care about him?—he's hardly in the story at all. But I noticed the repeated differentiation at the story's beginning between men and women, and the put-downs of women. The story seemed to be set-ting me up for some attitude toward women, and even though I noticed this, I did take the attitude: women are mean, ill-willed, and therefore (though not men's equals) menacing. Miss Emily is menacing. But at first she seems grotesque and stupid: her house smells bad; she's fat, with a dead look; she faces down the fathers [i.e. the aldermen] by (apparently) missing their point. Only gradually do I see the force of her will, that just because she doesn't go out or *do* anything doesn't mean that she isn't in control.

The scene with the rat-poison is crucial here: Miss Emily got her way, and the fact that her way is inscrutable, though surely menacing (arsenic), only makes it worse. The whole feeling of the story is of a mystery, something to do with male-female relationships, as well as time, perhaps, but a mystery one doesn't entirely want solved. Perhaps because I knew what was coming my mind wandered, putting even further distance between myself and the dis-gusting (but fascinating) revelation of the "bedroom" scene at the end. But the distancing is there in the story itself. The time-lags, the mysteriousness, the indirection, all put barriers between you and the story's subject.

So this is what I'd say at first reading, anyway. As far as response goes, mine is a considerable *fear* of the discovery I know is waiting, the sex-and-death thing, though there is a *fascination,* too. As far as the story's technique goes, I think it sets up shields of various sorts, that hide the ultimate truth, yet that have chinks that give us inklings, and the effect of secrets-not-entirely-hidden, of horrible-premonitions-defended-against, is what I'd guess is the technique that seems to arouse my feelings.

Now let me admit, right off, that this isn't an "unmediated" response to Faulkner's story. It was written not during but immediately after reading the story, by a relatively sophisticated, self-conscious reader, who also had some foreknowledge of the story's shocking climax. Most of all, it is a *written account* of a response, and so subject to all kinds of misrepresentation on my part *as I wrote it.* Also it was written by someone who has had considerable exposure to psychotherapy, and who therefore is somewhat at ease when expressing a taboo pleasure at contemplating necrophilia, an activity that is widely considered (and no doubt really is) loathsome to engage in.

Nonetheless, all this said, my response should give comfort to literary Freudians. For what I saw in "A Rose for Emily" was pretty certainly a "primal scene." Both my fear and my interest, my loathing and pleasure, derived, at least in part, from remembered childish speculation as to what went on in the parental bedroom. The structure of the story's plot is to set up a dark and impenetrable mystery—what is troubling Emily?—and to penetrate deeper and deeper into her past in hopes of getting an answer. Formally the pleasure is derived from solving the mystery, but the solution is a shocking one. My unconscious *knew* all along that nothing good went on behind a locked bedroom door, but now it has proof, and has won a victory over my conscious mind, which assured me it was none of my business. My conscious mind, meanwhile, has to content itself with solving a puzzle, with the self-evident reflection that after all Emily and Homer aren't Mom and Dad, and that, anyway, "it's only a story."

Beyond the illicit pleasure of letting a taboo thought become momentarily conscious, there was more bad news for my conscious mind in my response to "A Rose for Emily," for it turns out that my unconscious is a nasty little sexist, as I dutifully though rather reluctantly reported in my journal: "women are mean, ill-willed, men's inferiors, and menacing." I don't approve of such feelings, or consciously agree with them—some of my best friends are women—but they are *there* lying in wait for me when I read

Faulkner. My shocked response to the imagined scene of Emily bedding down with Homer Barron's decomposing body, and my related interest at male/female antagonism and conflict in the story are only the beginnings of an interpretation, of course, but any class I would teach, or essay I would write on the story would feature such interests prominently.

In sharp contrast to my response was that of my student, Stacy. Since her notebook remained in her possession, I will summarize from memory her entry on "A Rose for Emily." Surprisingly, Stacy did not mention the terrible denouement of the story—the discovery of Homer Barron's remains in Emily's bed. On questioning, she said that Emily's poisoning of Homer remained shadowy and hypothetical in her mind, and she had completely missed the implication of the strand of Emily's hair found on the pillow next to the corpse. Instead, Stacy had written a rather poetic reverie about her *grandmother*, of whom she was strongly reminded by Emily. The grandmother lived, Stacy wrote, shut away in a house full of relics and mementos of the past. Events of long ago, and people long dead, were more real to her than the world of the present, but Stacy found very positive things in her grandmother, and (by implication) in Emily as well: endurance, faith, love. She even identified the frail, pretty woman with Faulkner's picture of Emily when young: "a slender figure in white."

The contrast between our two reactions to the story was striking, and cause for discussion in class. In a more conventional course, I might have been tearing my hair over a student who so "missed the point" of the story as to ignore in her interpretation the terrifying climax of Emily's story, and who did not even notice the grizzly implications of that strand of iron-grey hair on the pillow beside Homer Barron. But what I found myself doing, instead, was to go back over the story and see how much of its meaning *I* had missed, how much there was in Faulkner's picture of Emily that *was* attractive, noble, tragic. Deprived of all normal suitors by a domineering father, she had clung to that father, even in death; deprived of her father, she had found a suitor outside the limits of respectability for a woman of her class and background; threatened with his loss as well she found a way to keep him, and then she remained true to him all the days of her life. Certainly it is hard entirely to like a Juliet who poisons her Romeo, yet remember that this is an extraordinarily evasive, indirect story, in which the reader can easily overlook unwanted implications. No poisoning actually occurs in its pages; the deed is left for the reader to infer. Stacy found it easy to ignore, and when confronted with it, accepted it as a qualification, but not a refutation of her admiration for Emily: just as I was able to modify my interpretation of the story without giving up my spontaneous horror, so Stacy could acknowledge the horror, without surrendering her view of Emily as embodying positive values.

What happened between Stacy and me is a perfectly familiar event in the lives of all of us: we communicated our differing interpretations to each other and both learned from the exchange. I wasn't right and she wrong, nor *vice versa*. Nor did we emerge from the exchange with identical interpretations of the story: Emily will doubtless never be as noble a character for me as she is for Stacy. Nonetheless, each of us improved his or her sense of understanding the story by sharing it with the other. Similarly, I can imagine no essay that I might read on "A Rose for Emily" that would leave my sense of the story entirely unchanged, nor any essay that would completely obliterate my old sense of the story. Meaning, as David Bleich has so eloquently argued, is constituted by individual readers as response, and is then negotiated by them into group knowledge. Readers, first individually and then collectively, make meaning.

Now what, we might want to ask, must Faulkner's text be like, if Stacy's interpretation and mine are both "right"—both defensible, that is, under the laws of logic and evidence? The obvious answer is that the text must be ambiguous. Indeed we have already seen its ambiguity with reference to Emily's own character. A figure of pathos as a young girl under her father's thumb, she develops in later years into a formidable figure herself. Victimized first by her father and then by Homer Barron, she turns the tables and becomes a victimizer; but even in this latter role she is ambiguous—the villainous-heroic resolver of an impossible situation. Even physically our imaginations must hover between the picture of Emily as a slender, girlish, angelic creature, and that of the older Emily: "She looked bloated, like a body long submerged in motionless water, and of that pallid hue." To complicate matters still further, the advanced-age description occurs earlier in the story.

The ambiguities of Emily's character are echoed in those of the other people portrayed in the story. The fact is that, like Emily, all characters in this story are seen through such a veil of vagueness, of mysteriousness, of innuendo pointing in no clearly defined direction, that whatever stance a reader takes toward any of the characters is conjecture based on little real information.

Equally vague and contradictory are the subjects and themes that we find in the story. Take the issue that spoke to me most at first reading: the man/woman polarity. The narrator (although typically given no name, age, sex, or other distinguishing characteristic) begins in the first sentence to distinguish between the sexes:

> When Miss Emily Grierson died, our whole town went to her funeral: the men through a sort of respectful affection for a fallen monument, the women mostly out of curiosity to see the inside of her house. . . .

In contrast to women, men seem high-minded here, capable of a gallantry echoed in Judge Stevens' refusal to force Emily to clean her house: "'Dammit, sir,' Judge Stevens said, 'will you accuse a lady to her face of smelling bad?'" When Emily begins her "affair" with Homer Barron (the exact nature of which is, to put it mildly, unclear) it is "the ladies" who try to meddle, while "the men did not want to interfere." Struggle is certainly there between men and women, but my initial interpretation of the story as "bad woman destroys good man" suppresses a good deal of evidence that it is the men, father and lover, who are ultimately responsible for Emily's pitiful condition. If she later turns the tables on them and wins a series of victories, isn't this an instance of the underdog triumphing? Emily's "victories" are, in any case, utterly grotesque (she succeeds in buying arsenic from the reluctant druggist, she succeeds in "keeping" her faithless lover) and could as easily be called *moral defeats*. If there is a battle of the sexes in "A Rose for Emily," the reader must decide who wins.

Other polarities are equally ambiguous. The story sets up tensions— or allows tensions to be felt—between age and youth, parent and child, black and white, individual and group, North and South, past and present, love and hate, and perhaps most of all between life and death. The picture (not actually in the story, but imperatively implied by it in my experience) of "bloated" corpselike Emily lying with her decomposing lover is as vivid an image of death-in-life as I know: Emily already dead in a sense, Homer still alive to her (despite the stink, the "fleshless grin"). Which one of them is deader? Which one would you rather be? Nowhere in literature do I remember the line between death and life so definitively rubbed out.

Indeed, I find it tempting to picture Faulkner's story as a series of widening concentric rings, with the dead/alive lovers at their center. As we move outward, we reach progressively wider polarities: the family (Emily/Father), the community (individual/group; men/women; older/younger generations), the nation (North/South: "And now Miss Emily had gone to join the representatives of those august names where they lay in the cedar-bemused cemetery among the ranked and anonymous graves of Union and Confederate soldiers who fell at the battle of Jefferson"), and the universe (past/present; life/death). "What is true at the center," the story seems to say, "is equally true at every wider circumference." But what (I ask) is true at the center? Those lovers on their bed seem to be a hieroglyph of some profound truth about life, death, time—about *everything*, in fact. But any attempt to pin it down, to state its meaning, excludes other equally possible interpretations—which doesn't mean that we shouldn't interpret, but only that we should have some humility about the status of our results.

Finally, with respect to the story's technique, we find the same sort of ambiguities. I mentioned in my original journal entry the extraordinary indirection with which the story is told. The narrator is anything but omniscient, reporting only what is common knowledge in Jefferson, and even then withholding foreknowledge of earlier events—such as the cause of the bad smell emanating from Emily's house in the months following Homer's disappearance—until the right moment comes to spring it on the reader.

The narrator is himself a "reader" of Emily's story, trying to put together from fragments a complete picture, trying to find the meaning of her life in its impact upon an audience, the citizens of Jefferson, of which he is a member. He disregards chronology, working generally backward from recent events to ever-earlier ones, as if seeking their explanation in a receding past that never throws quite enough light. Displaced chronology and the narrator's carefully limited point of view are two sources of the story's murkiness, which leaves us constantly guessing about events—What caused the smell? Why did Emily buy arsenic? What happened to Homer? Yet the narrator can be wonderfully, or cruelly, explicit too in his handling of details.

To read Faulkner's story, then, is to negotiate a series of oppositions that the text itself has left unresolved. We feel compelled to resolve its ambiguities, but however we do so, some of the evidence will have to be ignored. Small wonder if Stacy and I each constructed our interpretations out of different bits of this conflicting, shifting, and incomplete mass of evidence, each of us ignoring what didn't fit.

It is often argued, when this point is reached, that the text in question is in a special (though daily widening) category of texts whose meaning is, in effect, "everything is ambiguous." Modern critics—New Critical, Structuralist, semiotic, deconstructive—are fond of finding this message everywhere they look. I confess a fondness for it myself, yet I remember that at first "A Rose for Emily" had a definite meaning for me; that only second, more "mature" thoughts softened it into a structure of irresolvable ambiguities. I am not convinced, in other words, that ambiguity is the *meaning* of Faulkner's story. I think, rather, that it is the *nature* of this text to be ambiguous, and that meaning is what the reader makes, by choosing among its paired, antithetical elements. I hope to have demonstrated this contention with respect to "A Rose for Emily." I cannot hope to prove here, but do affirm my belief that all literary texts are by nature ambiguous, and that the reader makes their meaning.

In his extensive inquiry into the psychology of reading, *5 Readers Reading*, Norman Holland asks what is the nature of a text, and then shrugs his shoulders:

> A reader reads something, certainly, but if one cannot separate his "subjective" response from its "objective" basis, there seems no way to find out what that "something" is in any impersonal sense. It is visible only in the psychological processes the reader creates in himself by means of the literary work. (p. 40)

Certainly Holland has a point: it is impossible to discover a situation in which a text can be observed without an observer (a reader) being present. Yet it is well to remember that this predicament is shared by all the sciences, even by particle physics, which nonetheless goes on finding leptons and quarks, the sub-subatomic particles of matter. Moreover, if it is impossible to describe the *text* with certainty, that same limitation applies, in spades, to describing with certainty the reader's "psychological processes"—approximation and plausibility are the most we can hope for in either enterprise.

Holland writes as if a solitary reader confronted a solitary text in a void, equipped only by the internal psychological processes described by Freud. This is for Holland a fruitful hypothesis; yet, from another, equally sound, point of view, the individual reader is a member of a society, a product of a lifetime of education whose substance is the learning of conventions shared by other members of society. The very language in which the literary text is written is the product not of his own psyche but of a human community ongoing over millennia. It seems clear that the individual reader reads, in part at least, according to conventions, strategies, and expectations that he has learned from other human beings and that he shares with them.

Remember, for example, that though Stacy and I interpreted Emily in antithetical ways, we both shared a reading strategy: call it reading-for-character. It would seem that the text could accordingly be described as embodying the "character-reading code," put there by Faulkner, who knew the code as well as anyone. This is the approach of the relatively new discipline of Semiotics, whose goal is to specify all the codes operating in a text and thus to read "scientifically." In practice, though, the name and nature of the codes are variable with the critic and the work, and the codes become so numerous and so redundant that instead of achieving with their help a specific meaning we are left, once again, contemplating the universal aesthetic message of ambiguity.

We are on firmer ground, I think, when we think of the "codes" as in the reader, not in the text, and call them "reading conventions" or "reading strategies." Stacy and I (and many others) read "A Rose for Emily" as a portrait of its heroine's character, but that's not *all* we read it as, and other readers will apply entirely different strategies: the Marxist will read for (and find) representations of a decaying class-structure and social victimization, a deconstructionist will read it as a self-consuming artifact, allegorizing readers of all sorts will read for all sorts of symbols, a Structuralist will read for structures; and in no case (except perhaps by majority-rule) can we exclude any of these strategies from validity, though some will interest us more than others.

But if the "codes" are in the reader, what is in the text? I suggest that when we look closely at texts what we find are not "codes"—consistent, coherent, smoothly concatenated—but a jumble of "features" or "elements." The maddening thing is that these elements seem to spring into being only when a reader is present—that is, when a reading strategy is being applied. The reader's freedom is limited both by the elements in the story, and by the codes he has learned from his culture, but since he *is* free to select which codes he applies, which elements he constitutes, he is in practice no more constrained by them than putting on a pair of sneakers compels me to run. What he *is* forced to do is to apply *some* strategy, look at *some* elements of the text (since that, after all, is what reading is) and in so doing he joins a community of which all other readers, and the author himself, are members—he enters, that is, a dialogue, all of whose voices speak within him, all of whose roles he plays.

It is my conclusion—a tentative conclusion, as always—that such issues are never definitively settled; that since literary texts are richly ambiguous, individual readers do resolve those ambiguities, fill in the hermeneutic gaps, with their own individual psychological makeups, their own "identity themes," to borrow Holland's phrase. But reader and text do not exist in a void. Rather, they are framed by a vast series of linguistic, literary, and cultural conventions of interpretation, some of which, at least, readers cannot help knowing and using, since that is what "reading" is. These conventions, or codes, are *so* numerous, however, and so mutually contradictory, that the individual reader still exercises considerable freedom in the way he interprets, merely by his choice and emphasis among the conventions.

Reading is *both* a solitary *and* a communal enterprise; we read *both* for self-discovery *and* to learn about the world; and we go on learning, after we have read a text, by sharing our interpretation with others, and by letting their interpretations enrich our own.

I won't pretend that disagreements, even violent disagreements, can't occur. Many of them are due to the pernicious belief in "right reading": the idea that if you and I disagree, one of us is wrong, and it better not be me! But disagreements can also result from real moral or political differences. Even here, though, negotiation and compromise may be a more useful approach than the verbal equivalent of war, however stimulating and entertaining a quarrel may be.

Still, it helps to remember that these disagreements are not epistemological but political, whether on or off the campus. I had only to *offer* my interpretation of "A Rose for Emily" for Stacy to change hers, but if she had resisted mine completely, I would still have listened to hers and learned from it, confident that sooner or later she would follow my example. Telling her that she was "wrong" would have been not only unhelpful but untrue. Her interpretation was *not* wrong; it was merely partial, incomplete, and *all* interpretations are incomplete. Literary study *is* a discipline not because it gives *certain* answers—no field of inquiry does that—but because it is eternally in the business of developing procedures for assembling evidence and answering questions about an area of human experience that human beings collectively judge to be important and worthy of inquiry. Literary theory, I submit, is nothing more nor less than the study, with regard to literary texts, of how readers make meaning.

NOTES

1 "How Readers Make Meaning" is a sequel to my earlier article ("Do Readers Make Meaning?") printed in *The Reader in The Text: Essays on Audience and Interpretation,* Susan R. Suleiman and Inge Crosman, eds. (Princeton: Princeton University Press, 1980), pp. 149–64. "How Readers" was delivered in an earlier form to the Theories of Reading Conference sponsored by the Society For Critical Exchange and Indiana University and held in Bloomington on 28–30 September 1981.

Those acquainted with "reader-response" theories will recognize, throughout my essay, bits and pieces of the ideas and methods of Norman Holland, David Bleich, Wolfgang Iser, Jonathan Culler, and Stanley Fish, and of Structuralism ("binary opposition"), Semiotics ("codes"), and deconstruction (Derrida: "the reader writes the text"). Those for whom these names and slogans are not household words will find a useful, 23-page bibliography by Inge Crosman in Suleiman and Crosman. More on these matters will also be found in my essay "The Twilight of Critical Authority," *Annals of Scholarship* 1, 1 (Winter, 1980) and in the first chapter of my book *Reading Paradise Lost* (Bloomington: Indiana University Press, 1980).

SUZANNE HUNTER BROWN

"A Rose for Emily," by William Faulkner

Here we will consider some aspects of the critical tradition surrounding William Faulkner's "A Rose for Emily" in order to see how the criticism reflects and embodies the tension between sequence and configuration, between global and local processing, which I have described as central to the short story. I assume, as does Dieter Freundlich in his analysis of interpretations of Poe's tales, that "one major aspect of the analysis of interpretations, rather than literary texts themselves, is an explanation of how ascriptions of global meanings to texts come about." This approach emphasizes the ways in which reader perception underlies both the meaning of individual texts and a useful definition of genre. As Marie-Laure Ryan writes: "Once we realize that genres are a matter of communication and signification, generic taxonomy becomes tied to the same type of assumption that underlies current linguistic theories: namely that the object to account for is the user's knowledge. . . . The significance of generic categories thus resides in their cognitive and cultural value, and the purpose of genre theory is to lay out the implicit knowledge of the users of genre."[1]

I have chosen Faulkner's story, a war horse of high school anthologies, for two reasons. First, we have a tremendous body of material recording and analyzing the responses of various readers to the text. This material covers not only the views of professional literary critics but also those of presumably less experienced readers.[2] Second, the text is self-reflexive. Faulkner comments within it on the possible ways in which readers may organize the information provided and implies the ways in which various interpretive strategies may affect meaning.

The narrator of "A Rose for Emily" contrasts a reading of Miss Emily's story which emphasizes chronology with one which does not. He comments explicitly on the way in which the old men who attend the heroine's funeral view her past and their own. These Civil War veterans talk of Miss Emily as if she had been a contemporary, "believing that they had danced with her and courted her perhaps, confusing time with its mathematical progression, as the old do, to whom all the past is not a diminishing road, but, instead, a huge meadow which no winter ever quite touches, divided from them now by the narrow bottleneck of the most recent decade of years." This quotation suggests Faulkner's preoccupation in his famous story with the way in which interpreters — the southern townsmen, Miss Emily, the narrator of the story, and, finally, the readers of the text—construct Miss Emily's story. Faulkner opposes two alternatives: a linear, sequential organization ("a diminishing road") and a configurational, spatial patterning ("a huge meadow"). As Dennis Allen observes, "In contrast to the 'diminishing road' of chronological time, memory is nonlinear, a space in which the present and the various areas of the past exist simultaneously, eternally immune from death and decay."[3] Each interpreter of Emily's story is caught between these two ways of making sense.

Other reader-response critics have already noted that the text depends on the foregrounding of achronological patterning to achieve one of its major effects, though they have not discussed the way in which the brevity of the short story form may reinforce Faulkner's careful control of the connections readers make. Menakhem Perry remarks that the surprise ending would scarcely be a surprise if readers ordered the events in the story as a cause-and-effect sequence unfolding in time; if a reader put together that Homer Barron was heard to say he was not a marrying man, that Miss Emily then bought arsenic, that her lover was next seen entering her house at dusk and was never seen again, that shortly thereafter a terrible smell of decay appeared around her house, he might well have his suspicions long before he reads that the townspeople break open a sealed room after her funeral and discover the body she had slept beside. Perry notes that Faulkner deliberately scrambles the chronology of the *fibula* and substitutes analogical connections leading to perception of Miss Emily's qualities, her static "character," for those of time.[4] The episode in which Miss Emily buys the arsenic, for example, is introduced as an example of her imperviousness; it is like other occasions (regardless of time) when she demonstrates this same quality: "It was as if she demanded more than ever the recognition of her dignity as the last Grierson; as if it had wanted that touch of earthiness to reaffirm her imperviousness. Like when she bought the rat poison, the arsenic." Similarly, the incident of the smell is linked by analogy to an incident many years afterwards: "So she vanquished them, horse and foot, just as she had vanquished their fathers thirty years before about the smell."

Although Perry's article supplies a valuable analysis of the foregrounding of configurational links instead of sequential ones, Perry does not fully consider that it is the narrator of the story who supplies these achronological connections. Most critics see the story's unusual point of view as highly significant. Faulkner's narrator uses the pronoun *we*, emphasizing his role as a spokesman for the town and insisting that his information about the heroine is assembled from the gossip around Jefferson. It is this embodiment of town opinion that suppresses the sequential unfolding of Miss Emily's story. If Faulkner's sole purpose were to distract the reader from his surprise ending, he would be singularly unsuccessful. Junior high school students may indeed be pleasantly shocked by Miss Emily's crime, but for years my college students have reported that they saw through the whole affair early on (though they may still be surprised by the infamous strand of hair). Compared to Agatha Christie, Faulkner, then, is a failure. He seems almost to be colluding with the reader behind the back of the dull narrator, who ignores the significance of chronology. In each of the two cases cited above, after the narrator has emphasized the timeless nature of Miss Emily's character, he presents the reader with the significant timing of the event, though the narrator himself seems not to catch on: "That was over a year after they had begun to say 'Poor Emily,' and while the two female cousins were visiting her" (the purchase of the poison) and "That was two years after her father's death and a short time after her sweetheart—the one we believed would marry her—had deserted her" (the smell).

In fact, the narrator, and by extension the people of Jefferson, are not dull, but are deliberately repressing time and sequence when they consider Miss Emily. Throughout the story, the narrator compares Miss Emily to timeless and immortal symbols. She is a "fallen monument," an "angel in a colored church window," a "strained flag," an "idol in a niche." It is he who offers the "rose" for Emily, the story, which, unlike real roses, cannot fade and die. No wonder the townspeople are shocked; no wonder they have the story all wrong until they break open the door of her chamber and discover that the last Grierson was also a mortal woman existing in time. The townspeople's suppression of sequence in Miss Emily's story is linked to their static view of history. As Allen points out, the townspeople "not only recognize the social taxonomy but actively work to maintain it," since it is they who call in the Alabama cousins when they believe their monument is "fallen."[5] They are understanding of, even pleased by, Miss Emily's more dramatic demonstrations of her "Griersonness." In her, they find the unnatural natural; the narrator says of her denial of her father's death: "We believed she had to do that . . . [W]e knew that with nothing left, she would have to cling to that which had robbed her, as people will." Not only do the townspeople find that her status necessitates her denial of mortality; they are not surprised by her repression of sexuality. They expect her to marry Homer after the departure of the cousins, but when he disappears and she closets herself in the house, the narrator says, "We knew that this was to be expected too; as if that quality of her father which had thwarted her woman's life so many times had been too virulent and too furious to die."

But these statements also suggest that the townspeople are simultaneously aware of the sequential nature of Miss Emily's story: she has been "robbed" and "thwarted." Besides seeing her as the last Grierson, they see her as a young girl who has been denied suitors by her father and has then lost that father through death. She may have been a Grierson in the past, but she has now become a poor woman. When they think of her sequential history and not of her eternal status as a monument, the townspeople feel pity: "Poor Emily." Furthermore, this sequential reading of Miss Emily's story is linked to a progressive view of history and, as Allen points out, a new democratic ideology. The townspeople are pleased when Miss Emily becomes like them in knowing "the old thrill and the old despair of a penny more or less," the ladies are not surprised when the smell of decay links "the gross, teeming world and the high and mighty Griersons," and they are pleased when they believe Miss Emily has married the "Yankee day laborer"—thus, Allen claims, siding "with Emily's recognition of her sexuality, the sign of her similarity to her neighbors."[6] What they do not see is their own role in "robbing" and "thwarting" Miss Emily through their ambivalence about her status as icon.

The younger generation of townspeople is allied with the forces of progress. Indeed, the town has adapted to the gasoline pumps, cotton gins, and other "eyesores" of modern industrialism that Faulkner describes with distaste. The new generation is more interested in a dollar than in preserving Miss Emily's symbolic exemption from taxes. Yet it is precisely because the townspeople refuse to live in the past that they need a symbol of that past. Ambivalent about their own alliance with Yankee industrialism, they project all of their longing for the southern past onto the last Grierson. As Allen remarks, "If they are delighted by evidence that Emily is equal to them, this is because they do not wholly believe it."[7] Yet Faulkner does not allow the reader to sentimentalize that past as the townspeople do. The gracious Colonel Sartoris may seem more attractive than the introducers of more modern ideas, but it is he who "fathered the edict that no Negro woman would appear on the streets without an apron." The verb *fathered* is significant; while aware of the virtues of aristocratic agrarian paternalism, Faulkner shows in stories like "Barn Burning" that he can also be critical of that system. Sentimentalizing their past and their landowning class, the modern townspeople are also "clinging to that which had robbed them, as people will." Faulkner suggests that embracing the present while sentimentalizing the past as a dead symbol falsifies and perverts both.

Miss Emily is also caught between a static view of her enduring "Griersonness" and her sense of herself as an aging woman. She in part accepts the town's definition of her symbolic status. That she at first only accepts this interpretation is suggested by the narrator's comment on her acceptance of another "story," Colonel Sartoris' dispensation freeing her from taxes: "Only a man of Colonel Sartoris' generation and thought could have invented it, and only a woman could have believed it." She allows her father to drive away the young men who are not "good enough" to marry her and then denies his death. The insult of Homer's desertion after she has "lowered" herself from her status as southern lady leaves her with her "Griersonness"— "that quality of her father which had thwarted her woman's life so many times" and which "had been too virulent and too furious to die." The murder itself is, from Miss Emily's point of view, the supreme act which denies sequence at several levels: she brings together her earlier Oedipal attachment to her father and her later passion for Homer, she preserves Homer from death and change, and she negates her sexual "fill" and regains her status as icon through this "marriage." Only after she has killed Homer does she accept the town's repudiation of her life as a mortal woman who ages and "smells"; she grows fat and desexed, with hair a "vigorous iron-gray, like the hair of an active man," and sleeps with a corpse she can possess forever.

Miss Emily's affair with Homer Barron—a Yankee, a day laborer determined to escape the respectability of marriage—is her one attempt to assert her "woman's life." As many critics have pointed out, her choice of suitor is an active rejection of her status as an icon, the southern lady. She steps actively out of the frozen tableau in which her father blocks access to her with a horsewhip. Miss Emily, like the townspeople who first call in her relatives and then help her hoodwink them, does not fully accept the simultaneous, configurational reading of her life. Her involvement with Homer brings her into conflict with those who see her only as an eternal Grierson, the Alabama cousins. Even while she denies the passage of time and tells the town officials to consult Colonel Sartoris after he has been dead for years, a gold watch ticks at her side. And in contrast to the "immortal" rose, the tribute of art, is her rose room "decked and furnished as for a bridal," with curtains "of faded rose color" and with "rose-shaded lights," a room suggestive of her "woman's life" which exists in time and can decay. The appearance of this "rose" at the end of the story is the final reminder of Miss Emily's sequential reading of her own story.

Miss Emily's critics can be—and have been—classified in a number of different ways. The division explicitly raised in the text is between those who see the heroine's story as constituting a sequence and those, like the narrator and the townspeople, who subordinate chronology in favor of some "timeless" or otherwise symbolic reading. The latter are far more numerous.

These readers, like the narrator, emphasize the timeless traits of Miss Emily's supposedly unchanging character, though some find her "noble" and others "terrible." Cleanth Brooks and Robert Penn Warren merge these two responses in a single reading of Miss Emily's "character": "Perhaps the horrible and the admirable aspects of Miss Emily's final deed arise from the same basic fact of her character: she insists on meeting the world on her own terms." A slight variation on the reading-for-character strategy is provided by those psychological critics, such as Edward Stone, who see Miss Emily's course set once and for all by her relationship with her father: "Her passionate, almost sexual relationship with her dead father forces her to distrust the living body of Homer and to kill him so that he will resemble the dead father she can never forget."[8] For other critics, Miss Emily is a timeless symbol, as she is for the narrator. Early critical responses to the story often portray the heroine as the embodiment of the Old South, in opposition to the new generation of townspeople, the New South, influenced by and in tune with the Yankees (represented by Homer).[9]

Critics generally supply a configurational interpretation of the text, but they often display a competing awareness of Miss Emily's story as that of an individual life unfolding in time. Allen portrays Miss Emily as a static sign: "Both grotesquely fat and excessively thin, living and dead, female and male, Miss Emily is, finally, 'undecidable,' the co-presence of opposites." Thus Allen eradicates sequence in Miss Emily's story in the same way that he claims she is trying to do. Not surprisingly, this interpretive strategy leads him to deny the historicity of the tale and to view it as the embodiment of a timeless, universal conflict: "The story explores aristocratic and democratic perspectives, seen less as local, historical entities than as conflicting ideologies. . . . At a more basic level, the story suggests, the conflict is between two human tendencies: the impulse to identify differences and to erect taxonomies and the contrary desire to deny distinctions."[10]

Although Allen finally opts for this interpretation—which suppresses narrative development and thus causality—as the "basic" one, he is aware of the story's narrative aspects. Indeed, he quotes Faulkner's own comments on the story only to dismiss them as "not particularly helpful." Far from being "diverse, faintly contradictory, and often vague," as Allen calls them, Faulkner's explanations as interpreted by Allen actually construct the story as a sequential cause-and-effect narrative in which a conflict is resolved in terms of action: "Emily murders Homer *because* he 'was about to quit her'; the story explores 'the *conflict* of conscience with glands,' the 'Old Adam,' and Emily's expiation for breaking 'the laws of her tradition'; Emily's actions *result from* her father's repression of her 'normal aspirations' for love."[11] The interesting questions here are why Allen foregrounds the configurational interpretation and why he finds Faulkner's explanations unsatisfying.

Robert Crosman, in "How Readers Make Meaning," records his own growing awareness of the sequential possibilities of Miss Emily's story. Like Allen, he originally organized the text as embodying contrasting signs and drew from this procedure a timeless "truth": "But I noticed the repeated differentiation at the story's beginning between men and women, and the put-downs of women. The story seemed to be setting me up for some attitude toward women, and even though I noticed this, I did take the attitude: women are mean, ill-willed, and therefore (though not men's equals) menacing." Challenged by a female student's admiration for Miss Emily, Crosman saw "how much there was in Faulkner's picture of Emily that was attractive, noble, tragic."[12]

Interestingly, in his reevaluation, Crosman emphasizes the gross sequence of events he reconstructed from the story: "Deprived of all normal suitors by a domineering father, she had clung to that father, even in death; deprived of her father, she had found a suitor outside the limits of respectability for a woman of her class and background; threatened with his loss as well she found a way to keep him, and then she remained true to him all the days of her life." Like the townspeople, Crosman is considerably more sympathetic to Miss Emily when he considers her story as a sequence of narrative events: "Poor Emily." This view of Miss Emily's character emphasizes development, not any "basic fact of her character" (Brooks and Warren) or static embodying of opposing traits (Allen): "A figure of pathos as a young girl under her father's thumb, she *develops* in later years into a formidable figure *herself.* Victimized *first* by her father and *then* by Homer Barron, she turns the tables and *becomes* a victimizer." Despite these readings that emphasize narrative sequence, Crosman returns to viewing the text as composed of "paired, antithetical elements," not mentioning that some of these elements follow others (either in the text or in an inferred event chain) and may be caused by them.[13]

Why do so many critics join the narrator in suppressing the sequential nature of Miss Emily's story? Why do they, like the townspeople, rush to reestablish her as a symbol or a sign? Those early critics who see her as a symbol of the Old South are very close to reading her story as the townspeople do, and even later critics who reject this view employ essentially the same way of organizing the text, processing it locally and sorting minimal units (details, even individual words) into polarized oppositions, emphasizing similarity and difference and ignoring sequence. This is especially odd because the text itself has emphasized the faulty or, at best, partial reading of the story which results from this interpretive process; we have seen that the narrator's preference for analogical rather than sequential associations prevents him from "putting things together" in order to understand what has happened. But is it true that the narrator and the townspeople *haven't* put the sequential, cause-and-effect story together? That the narrator always mentions the significant timing of a remembered event immediately after substituting an achronological link is more suggestive of repression than of stupidity. When I ask my students if the townspeople know about Homer's murder, they generally say something like, "Well, the people in the town know there's something really wrong, but they don't consciously admit to themselves what they know." Such comments bear an interesting resemblance to Crosman's more graceful description of his experience of reading the story: "As far as response goes, mine is a considerable fear of the discovery I know is waiting."[14]

The discovery of the story's "shock" is the discovery of the possibility of organizing the text as a narrative sequence; the repression of the one is the repression of the other. The narrator and the reader share in Miss Emily's denial of sequence and her recognition of sequence, and *may* participate in her rerepression of temporal process by converting it to a simultaneous sign. Allen has described Miss Emily's behavior well, though he is more interested in her repression of the body than in her repression of time:

> By disposing of Homer, she is able to repudiate her sexuality; by preserving his corpse, she can deny the reality of death. Yet, as murder, her crime admits the existence of death just as her necrophilia acknowledges her sexual drives. . . . If sexuality and death cannot be excluded successfully from the aristocratic world, if Emily is forced to recognize them, they can be rerepressed; Emily's recognition itself will be repudiated. Thus Homer is consigned to the closed room upstairs that, as a combined bridal chamber/tomb, contains and circumscribes not simply sexuality and death but the entire process of biological existence, from the nuptial relations, which are its origin, to the grave, which is its end.[15]

In short, Miss Emily's move from victim to victimizer is also her conversion from acceptance of a role as symbol to performance of a role as sign maker and manipulator. Her affair with Homer is her attempt to liberate her physical life from the configurational reading assigned to it by her neighbors and accepted by herself; when this attempt fails, she decides that she will at least design and control the configuration by which the sequential nature of her existence is denied.

Throughout "A Rose for Emily" Faulkner plays with the tension between sequential and configurational organization characteristic of the short story form. He does so on several different levels. Within the story, the sequence of gross narrative events threatens to break through the configurational reading imposed by the narrator. The story is also "about" Miss Emily's own attempts to break the reading of her story as eternal configuration, an attempt that fails. The final level on which this tension is resolved is generic. The reader's disposition to continue pairing minimal semantic units in terms of similarity and difference rather than in terms of a sequence of gross narrative events is in part controlled by the text's brevity. I have argued elsewhere that perceiving a work as a short story creates a strong drive to render all details "symbolic," that is, to interpret them symbolically.[16] Not only does the reader seek to avoid the "horror" of the sequential discovery, but the psychological tendencies engendered by brevity help Faulkner mislead the reader. Moreover, "A Rose for Emily," unlike most short stories, makes it clear to the reader that a tendency to process the work as a configurational structure obscures another important way of interpreting the text. The story thus becomes Faulkner's exploration of the limitations of the form.

NOTES

[1] Dieter Freundlich, "Understanding Poe's Tales: A Schema-theoretic View," *Poetics*, XI (1982), 28, with the permission of North-Holland Publishing Company, Amsterdam; Marie-Laure Ryan, "On the Why, What and How of Generic Taxonomy," *Poetics*, X (1981), 111–12.

[2] This story has attracted the attention of a large number of critics concerned with reader response. See Norman Holland's *Five Readers Reading* (New Haven, 1975), which includes the responses of undergraduate English majors to the text.

[3] Dennis Allen, "Horror and Perverse Delight: Faulkner's 'A Rose for Emily,'" *Modern Fiction Studies*, XXX (1984), 688.

[4] Menakhem Perry, "Literary Dynamics: How the Order of a Text Creates Its Meanings," *Poetics Today*, I (Autumn, 1979), 35–64, 311–61.

[5] Allen, "Horror and Perverse Delight," 693.

[6] *Ibid.*, 692.

[7] *Ibid.*, 693.

[8] Cleanth Brooks and Robert Penn Warren, *Understanding Fiction* (New York, 1943), 413; Edward Stone, *A Certain Morbidness* (Carbondale, Ill., 1969), 96.

[9] See George Dillon, "Styles of Reading," *Poetics Today*, III (Spring, 1982), 85, for a discussion of this critical view.

[10] Allen, "Horror and Perverse Delight," 695.

[11] *Ibid.*, 686–87, emphasis mine.

[12] Robert Crosman, "How Readers Make Meaning," *College Literature*, IX (1982), 207–208, 209.

[13] *Ibid.*, 209, 210, 212, emphasis mine.

[14] *Ibid.*, 208.

[15] Allen, "Horror and Perverse Delight," 695.

[16] See Suzanne Hunter Brown, "'Tess' and *Tess*: An Experiment in Genre," *Modern Fiction Studies*, XXVIII (1982), 40.

JACK SCHERTING

Emily Grierson's Oedipus Complex: Motif, Motive, and Meaning in Faulkner's "A Rose For Emily"

Most readers of Faulkner's story "A Rose for Emily" would agree that its meaning is somehow connected with the motive which prompts Emily Grierson to poison her lover and conceal his corpse from the public for some forty years. Most readers would also agree that the problem of identifying this motive and relating it to the meaning of the story is complicated by the manner in which Faulkner has narrated his tale. "A Rose for Emily" is related by an anonymous narrator in the first person plural. Faulkner uses the "we" point of view to indicate that the events are being described by a resident of Jefferson[1]—a representative of the community's collective understanding of Emily's life. His desultory narrative, which incorporates a substantial amount of local gossip, is of necessity incomplete because Emily seldom left her house and because the only person who could have described what actually went on inside that house—her Negro servant—ran off immediately after her death. By limiting access to the facts this way, Faulkner forces the reader to search beyond the surface of the narrative for an explanation of Emily's behavior.

This is a formidable task because Faulkner, through his narrator, is obviously describing a psychotic personality. The narrator recognizes and comments perceptively on the superficial aspects of Emily's bizarre conduct, but he does not attempt to explain the nature of Emily's derangement nor is he able to offer a motive which would clear up the mystery. In this sense he is a naive raconteur. Moreover, his retrospective narration scrambles the chronology of the story, leaving readers with the task of reconstructing the sequence of events from casual references to time.

Much of the appeal of "A Rose for Emily" resides in the challenges which this mode of narration poses for anyone attempting to interpret the story. For assistance in untangling the chronology, readers can check Paul D. McGlynn's careful study[2]; but once this obstacle is surmounted, there remains the central question: Why did Emily Grierson murder her lover? This thematically significant question has not been satisfactorily answered. The generally accepted explanation was first proposed by Brooks and Warren: "Confronted with his jilting her, she tries to override not only his will and the opinion of other people, but the laws of death and decay themselves. . . . She would not be jilted."[3] This is an appealing explanation of Emily's motive, but it has one serious defect—the evidence contradicts rather than supports the assertion that Emily was jilted by her lover. A brief review of the evidence will show that this popular interpretation of motive has, at best, a weak factual basis.

Miss Emily and her lover, Homer Barron, had been carrying on for the better part of two years. We know this because Emily met Homer in the summer following her father's death and because the smell of Homer's decaying corpse was noticed about two years *after* her father died. During these two years, Homer visited Emily on a regular basis. This is evident in section 4 of the story, the first paragraphs of which summarize the townspeople's attitude toward Emily's conduct. At first they accepted her affair with benign tolerance, expecting it soon to be "ratified" by marriage. But when some two years had lapsed, tolerance gave way to indignation. The affair was temporarily interrupted during the visit of Emily's cousins, summoned by the minister's wife in a final effort to end the scandal.

If Faulkner had intended readers to infer that Homer Barron had jilted Emily or that he intended to jilt her, we would expect the author to provide some substantive evidence as a basis for such an inference. There is only one allusion to jilting in the history of this protracted affair. Noting Homer's disappearance, the people of Jefferson assumed that he "had deserted her. . . . after her sweetheart went away, people hardly saw her at all." That assumption is not reinforced anywhere else in the story. To the contrary, the evidence strongly suggests that Homer had *not* deserted her, that he was in fact taking a "long sleep" in an upstairs bedroom of the Grierson house: Emily purchased poison during her cousins' visit; Homer re-entered the Grierson house "within three days" of their departure and "that was the last we saw of Homer Barron"; "a short time after" Homer disappeared, a very disagreeable smell developed around the Grierson house; about forty years later, Homer's remains are discovered.

If, as the evidence suggests, Homer did not jilt Emily, what motive would she have for murdering him? To answer this question we need at least a glimpse into the recesses of her pathological mind. Unless Faulkner was simply presenting for us an incomprehensible mystery of demented behavior, he must, through his naive raconteur, have provided readers with the clues necessary to comprehend, however dimly, the contorted psyche which conceived and executed this singular murder/marriage. He did provide such clues. Deliberately and with consummate skill Faulkner employed the Freudian principle of Oedipal[4] fixation as a means of depicting Emily's character and informing the story with its powerful theme, a theme intimately connected with the incestuous nature of Emily's love for Homer. Emily Grierson was possessed by an unresolved Oedipal complex. Her libidinal desires for her father were transferred, after his death, to a male surrogate—Homer Barron. Fortunately we need not superimpose this Freudian structure on the story because there is ample evidence—external as well as internal—to show that Faulkner consciously used the Oedipal motif in composing his story.

First a look at the external evidence. Sigmund Freud's theories on sex had been pretty well assimilated (often half-digested) by the time "A Rose for Emily" was published in April of 1930. Like many other American authors, Faulkner was very much aware of and influenced by the literary possibilities inherent in the new psychological approach to maladjusted personalities.[5] In view of this, it seems curious that the relationship between Emily Grierson and her father has not been scrutinized with the care it deserves. In later years, Faulkner himself suggested the significance of that relationship, using a Freudian concept (repression) in his remarks [italics mine]:

> In this case there was a young girl with a young girl's *normal* aspirations to find love and then a husband and family, who was brow-beaten and kept down by her father, a selfish man who didn't want her to leave home because he wanted a housekeeper, and it was a *natural instinct* of—*repressed* which— you can't repress it—you can mash it down but it comes up somewhere else and very likely in a tragic form. . . .[6]

Because Faulkner stressed the significance of the father/daughter relationship, his comments should be given careful consideration. In doing so, I will paraphrase and analyze Faulkner's remarks in order to develop fully the meaning implicit in them. Emily's father had prevented her from maturing sexually in the normal and natural way. Thus repressed, her sexual drives emerged in a tragic form—that is to say, in abnormal and unnatural behavior. The affair between Emily and Homer is illicit, yes, but would Faulkner describe this situation—a situation in which a woman facing spinsterhood at last finds a lover—as tragic? Not likely. When he said that the repressed natural instinct comes up "somewhere else," he could only have meant somewhere *other than* a normal man/woman relationship. On the surface, Emily's affair with Homer falls well within the scope of sexual normalcy; however, if we start with the postulate that Emily was never allowed to outgrow her Oedipal attachment to her father and that Homer was, libidinally, a surrogate for her father, then the affair does indeed become abnormal and tragic. A closer look at the story itself will reveal the extent to which the Oedipal motif pervades Faulkner's tale.

Readers will recall that Emily's father—an imperious man, proud of his Southern heritage and of his family's status in Jefferson—had constantly interposed himself between Emily and any male interested in courting her. The narrator describes the situation in this way: "We had long thought of them as a tableau; Miss Emily a slender figure in white in the background, her father a spraddled silhouette in the foreground, his back to her and clutching a horsewhip, the two of them framed by the back-flung front door." Emily, already past thirty, had been denied normal contacts with the opposite sex. To use Freudian terminology, the father had prevented his daughter from transferring her libido to an outside object, thus intensifying her libidinal dependence upon him. Understandably, then, his death was an extremely traumatic event in her life—so traumatic that she could not consciously cope with it.

Emily's subsequent behavior clearly shows that the death of her father was a piece of reality disavowed by her ego. The narrator recalls that when neighbors came by to offer condolences the day after Mr. Grierson's death, "Miss Emily met them at the door, dressed as usual and with no trace of grief on her face. She told them that her father was not dead." For three days Emily guarded her father's corpse, turning away those who would take him from her. Finally, "just as they were about to resort to law and force, she broke down, and they buried her father quickly." Faulkner's use of the phrase "broke down" does not mean that Emily consciously acknowledged the reality of her father's death; on the contrary, her breakdown signalled a retreat from that reality into the defenses of her own psyche. Emily regressed into her childhood. This explains why she was "sick for a long time" after her father's death and why, during her seclusion, she cut her hair short, "making her look like a girl." Emily became an emotional orphan in search of the father who had been taken from her.

Through his narrator, Faulkner offered a key observation concerning Emily's relationship with her father and her refusal to give up his corpse: "We remembered all the young men her father had driven away, and we knew that with nothing left, she would have to cling to that which had robbed her, as people will." Indeed, Emily's father had robbed her of a normal sex life, preventing her from resolving the childhood Oedipal complex. And the people of Jefferson, in removing his corpse, had robbed her of the only man in her life. Under the circumstances, it is not at all surprising that Miss Emily's libidinal attachment to her father was soon transferred to a surrogate male.

In the summer following her father's death and Emily's long illness, Homer Barron—a Northerner—arrived in Jefferson and began work as a foreman of a sidewalk paving crew. Much to the surprise of the townfolk, Emily began an affair with Homer, an affair which lasted the better part of two years. Emily's conduct during that time baffled the people of Jefferson: How could she—a well-bred Southern lady—abide an intimate relationship with this common laborer, this Yankee? Though they "believed she had fallen," still Emily proudly "carried her head high" on her buggy rides with Homer each Sunday. This apparently inexplicable behavior becomes comprehensible when we recognize that Homer Barron is a surrogate for Emily's father. The deceased father was the *subject* of her sublimated desire, Homer merely the living *object* on which that desire had been fixed and from which she evidently received considerable gratification. Faulkner offers hints of this parallel between Mr. Grierson and Emily's lover. Both are characterized as strong-willed men, and in separate scenes, both are described holding horsewhips. Of greater significance, however, is the fact that Emily replaces the corpse of her father with that of his objective counterpart, Homer Barron. As we shall see later, Faulkner re-enforces this father/lover parallel by careful word choice and by ambiguous phrasing in the final scene.

We cannot, of course, unravel Emily's convoluted psyche and explain every aspect of her demented behavior. But it is evident that Emily perceives reality in a most peculiar way. She is unable to discriminate between a Southern gentleman and a Yankee laborer, between past and present, between sleep and death, between that which is vital and that which is decaying. With this background, we are in a position to examine more closely the motive which drove Emily to murder Homer and immure his corpse in the Grierson house for some forty years.

Emily's affair becomes complicated when the ladies of Jefferson, determined to end the scandal, encourage the Baptist minister to reason with Emily. Though we do not know what took place during his visit with Emily, we do know that the minister's efforts were futile and that he was somehow stunned by what he learned, for "he would never divulge what happened during that interview," and he "refused to go back again." The minister's wife then wrote to Emily's cousins in hopes that they would be able to deal with the deranged woman. Their arrival intensified rather than resolved Emily's problems. The narrator does not tell us what transpired during the cousins' brief visit with Emily. It was a private matter, and quite likely the people of Jefferson did not know the particulars. Obviously, however, what the cousins said precipitated a crisis in Emily's life, for she murdered her lover as soon as they left. We can only speculate on what they might have told her. Given the circumstances, it is logical to assume that they forced her to make a choice: either marry Homer or stop carrying on with him. If in fact they confronted Emily in this way, it would explain why she subsequently murdered her lover. Such a choice would place Emily in a terrible dilemma because "Homer himself had remarked . . . that he was not a marrying man." He preferred the male companionship of the local Elk's Club to the confines of the family circle. Still Emily could not bear parting with Homer, as society demanded, any more than she could bear parting with her beloved father. How did she respond when the security of her fragile universe was threatened in this way? The lover/father would not marry Miss Emily, so Emily took the initiative. She made preparations to marry Homer. During her cousins' visit, Emily purchased "a man's toilet set in silver, with the letters H. B. on each piece," as well as "a complete outfit of men's clothing, including a nightshirt." She also bought some arsenic.

Three days after Emily's cousins left, Homer returned to the Grierson house and remained there for some forty years. The people of Jefferson assumed that "he had deserted her," but Miss Emily had outsmarted them. She simultaneously murdered and "married" Homer Barron. Because the people of Jefferson had taken her beloved father's body from the Grierson house, Emily insured that they would not take away its surrogate by concealing, in an upstairs bedroom, the corpse of the man who gratified her unresolved Oedipal desires. Now he would never leave her bed; he would always be there to comfort her.

At the conclusion of his story, Faulkner re-enforces this connection between Emily's father and her lover. He does it first by using the word "profound" to suggest the parallel. Those who attended Emily's funeral some forty years after Homer's death saw a crayon portrait of her father "musing profoundly" over her coffin. And those who later entered the upstairs bedroom gazed upon Homer's remains, his skull confronting them with a "profound and fleshless grin." Why is this portrait of Emily's father, standing "on a tarnished gilt easel before the fireplace," mentioned at the beginning as well as at the end of the story? The portrait may have been the work of an ante-bellum artist; or it may be that Emily, who later took up china painting, did the portrait herself, using the antiquated crayon technique. Whatever the case may have been, the repeated reference to the portrait is an effective way of suggesting that the spirit of Mr. Grierson so preoccupied Emily's distorted universe that it dominated the personal identity of Homer Barron. The initials which Emily had ordered engraved on Homer's toilet set, a "wedding" gift, are now obscured by tarnish; what was once a face is now a featureless skull, heightening by contrast the lifelike image of her father standing vigil over Emily's coffin.

Another important key to the connection between Mr. Grierson and Homer Barron is contained in the ambiguity of a sentence which Faulkner carefully constructed. Commenting on Homer's fate, the narrator says, "Now the long sleep that outlasts love, that conquers even the grimace of love, had cuckolded him." One meaning of this sentence—the meaning understood by the narrator and the community he represents—is that death, the long sleep, has stolen Emily from Homer, that is, cuckolded him. But Faulkner's choice of phrases gives that sentence a second and far more significant meaning. To perceive this meaning we must remember that Emily could not distinguish sleep and death and that Homer Barron was merely a surrogate male who gratified her Oedipal desires. When placed against this background, the sentence can also be interpreted as follows: "The long sleep that outlasts love" refers to the interim—about forty-two years—between the death of her father and that of Emily. Even during this long sleep, Emily's father maintained the dominance over her sexuality which he had established in her formative years, outlasting by far Homer's two-year affair with his daughter. Faulkner's choice of the word "cuckold" also sheds light on this bizarre affair. Strange as it may seem, Homer Barron was cuckolded by Emily's deceased father every time he went to bed with her. And after Homer's death the spirit of Emily's ever-vigilant father, in some peculiar way, continued to live for Emily in the corpse she had lain with at least twice during her forty-year honeymoon.[7] This interpretation of the sentence is re-enforced by a second look at an earlier passage: "that quality of her father which had thwarted her woman's life so many times had been too virulent and too furious to die."

The title of Faulkner's story, like every facet of this carefully wrought gem, perfectly matches the overall design.[8] Roses had a definite symbolic meaning for couples and are still offered as a pledge of fidelity in passion. Though Emily slept with Homer and with his corpse in that rose-tinted bedroom, "furnished as for a bridal," yet she was psychically incapable of being unfaithful in her pathetic love for her own father. The rose symbol— by chance if not by design—can also be related to another meaning which helps to illuminate this dark side of Faulkner's tale. In ancient Rome, a rose suspended in a room signified that nothing which transpired *sub rosa* was to be divulged to the outside world. The Oedipal desires expressed in Emily's affair with Homer were never recognized by the people of Jefferson, and Emily herself was aware of them only as subconscious longings. This secret is inclosed within an intricately constructed story which, like a Chinese puzzle-box, challenges and at the same time frustrates our efforts to open it. Yet it is a secret which must be disclosed to appreciate the magnitude of Faulkner's achievement and the meaning of his story.

At this point, I feel obliged to apologize for my protracted analysis of the Oedipal motif inherent in "A Rose for Emily." Faulkner's story is of course not merely a case history of a pathological mind. I have treated the Oedipal motif in such detail to establish it as the primary vehicle which the author used to convey the broader meaning of his story. That meaning is inextricably bound to the incestuous nature of Emily's love affair with Homer and the necrophilia inherent in her relationship with Homer's corpse.

The elements of incest and necrophilia are not unique to this story: Faulkner treated them in works published before as well as after "A Rose for Emily," and in those works he used them as a device for commenting on what he felt were undesirable aspects of the Southern mentality. In *Go Down, Moses* (1942), for example, there are definite sociological implications in the fact that Lucius McCaslin begets a son on his own mulatto daughter. More to the point, however, is Faulkner's use of incest and necrophilia in *The Sound and the Fury*, published on October 7, 1929—just six months before "A Rose for Emily." Like Emily Grierson, Quentin Compson cannot adjust to the realities of the New South because he is so closely attuned to his ideal of the past—to the Old South, to what was dead and decayed. In Faulkner's words, Quentin "loved death above all . . . loved only death."[9] And like Emily Grierson, Quentin transfers this love of the past to a living object—his sister Caddy. His desire to preserve the purity of his distinguished family—and, by extension, his ideal of the past—manifests itself as an incestuous longing, unlike Emily's only in that he is conscious of the sin involved. Indeed, it is the sin itself rather than his sister which so attracted him, for Quentin . . .

> loved not his sister's body but some concept of Compson honor . . . loved not the idea of the incest which he could not commit, but some presbyterian concept of its eternal punishment: he, not God, could by that means cast himself and his sister both into hell, where he could guard her forever and keep her forevermore intact amid the eternal fires.[10]

The counterpart of Quentin's desire to preserve his ideal of the past is found in Emily's pathetic efforts to retain the corpse of her father and that of his surrogate, Homer Barron. Both Emily and Quentin try to subvert the reality of time and change: he by breaking his watch and committing suicide; she by denying progress and committing murder.

The ultimate responsibility for Emily's distorted sexuality rests on her father, for it was he, out of family pride, who had driven away all the young men because "none were quite good enough" to marry into the "high and mighty" Grierson family. It was he who dominated Emily's sexuality and conditioned her to idolize his moribund Southern values. The towering irony of it all is that the man through whom Emily physically expressed her love for her father and for all that he represented was a nobody from the North. The liaison between Emily and Homer was as sterile, as barren, as it could possibly be. In the Grierson family, Faulkner represents that element of Southern society which attempted to protect itself through isolation and to perpetuate its values through relationships which were fundamentally incestuous and inevitably debilitating. Unable to confront the realities of life in post-bellum America, that element of Southern society continued to cherish the corpse of a beloved but decayed ideal.

NOTES

[1] The narrator is evidently a male of about the same age as Emily. In section 4 of the story, paragraph two, a distinction is made between the attitude of the ladies and the men, the latter favoring non-intervention in Emily's affair. The narrator identifies himself with the male faction two paragraphs later: "we were all Miss Emily's allies to help circumvent the cousins." His first-hand knowledge of Emily's life indicates that he is about her age.

[2] "The Chronology of 'A Rose for Emily,'" *Studies in Short Fiction*, 6 (Summer 1969), 461–462.

[3] Cleanth Brooks and Robert Penn Warren, *Understanding Fiction* (2nd ed.; New York: F. S. Crofts, 1959), pp. 352; 354.

[4] The daughter/father relationship is often referred to as the Electra complex; however, for stylistic reasons I have employed the broader usage evident in Freud's discussions of Oedipal behavior.

[5] See William Richard Brown's doctoral dissertation "Faulkner's Use of the Materials of Abnormal Psychology in Characterization," University of Arkansas 1965.

[6] Frederick L. Gwynn and Joseph L. Blotner, eds., *Faulkner in the University* (Charlottesville: University of Virginia Press, 1959), p. 138.

[7] This assertion is based upon two elements of the story. In the first place, Homer's remains "had apparently once lain in the attitude of an embrace." In view of the tormenting

spasms associated with death by arsenic poisoning, Emily herself must have positioned Homer's corpse in this posture. Secondly, there is a "strand of iron-gray hair" found on the pillow next to the skeleton. The pillow has the "indentation of a head" and is covered by an even coating of dust. The fact that the strand of hair is iron-gray indicates almost certainly that Emily had also lain with Homer's remains, at least once, several years after his death. Emily's hair "was turning gray" when the townfolk saw her once again six months after Homer's disappearance. "During the next few years it grew grayer and grayer until it attained an even pepper-and-salt iron-gray, when it ceased turning." Since Emily's hair did not turn iron-gray until several years after Homer's death, that strand of hair found on the pillow could not have been left there earlier. Paul McGlynn ["The Chronology of 'A Rose for Emily'"] asserts that "Emily's hair turns gray during her six-month retreat after Homer's disappearance, so the strand of hair found on the pillow . . . has been there since the period between 1896 and 1898, the time from Homer's disappearance to the closing of the room." McGlynn overlooks the present continuous tense of the verb in Faulkner's phrase "was turning gray," concluding that Emily's hair had turned to the iron-gray shade of the strand found on the pillow. He also assumes that "Homer's bedroom has been closed for forty years. . . ." Granted, the narrator reports that "there was one room in that region above stairs which no one had seen in forty years," but this is an assumption on the narrator's part which is contradicted by his own facts. Emily had to have entered the room during that period; moreover, the strand of iron-gray hair and the "indentation of a head" on the pillow are the strongest possible evidence that she must have lain with Homer's corpse—how many times, we have no way of knowing. The fact that her pillow is found covered with dust indicates that she had ceased doing so sometime earlier.

⁸ Faulkner's response to a question about the meaning of the title was not particularly enlightening: "It was just 'A Rose for Emily'—that's all." (*Faulkner in the University*, p. 88.)

⁹ "Appendix: Compson." *The Sound and The Fury* (1929). New York: The Modern Library, 1992. 335.

¹⁰ Ibid.

JUDITH FETTERLEY

A Rose for
"A Rose for Emily"

In "A Rose for Emily" the grotesque reality implicit in Aylmer's idealization of Georgiana becomes explicit. Justifying Faulkner's use of the grotesque has been a major concern of critics who have written on the story. If, however, one approaches "A Rose for Emily" from a feminist perspective, one notices that the grotesque aspects of the story are a result of its violation of the expectations generated by the conventions of sexual politics. The ending shocks us not simply by its hint of necrophilia; more shocking is the fact that it is a woman who provides the hint. It is one thing for Poe to spend his nights in the tomb of Annabel Lee and another thing for Miss Emily

Grierson to deposit a strand of iron-gray hair on the pillow beside the rotted corpse of Homer Barron. Further, we do not expect to discover that a woman has murdered a man. The conventions of sexual politics have familiarized us with the image of Georgiana nobly accepting death at her husband's hand. To reverse this "natural" pattern inevitably produces the grotesque.

Faulkner, however, is not interested in invoking the kind of grotesque which is the consequence of reversing the clichés of sexism for the sake of a cheap thrill; that is left to writers like Mickey Spillane. (Indeed, Spillane's ready willingness to capitalize on the shock value provided by the image of woman as killer in *I, the Jury* suggests, by contrast, how little such a sexist gambit is Faulkner's intent.) Rather, Faulkner invokes the grotesque in order to illuminate and define the true nature of the conventions on which it depends. "A Rose for Emily" is a story not of a conflict between the South and the North or between the old order and the new; it is a story of the patriarchy North and South, new and old, and of the sexual conflict within it. As Faulkner himself has implied, it is a story of a woman victimized and betrayed by the system of sexual politics, who nevertheless has discovered, within the structures that victimize her, sources of power for herself. If "The Birthmark" is the story of how to murder your wife and get away with it, "A Rose for Emily" is the story of how to murder your gentleman caller and get away with it. Faulkner's story is an analysis of how men's attitudes toward women turn back upon themselves; it is a demonstration of the thesis that it is impossible to oppress without in turn being oppressed, it is impossible to kill without creating the conditions for your own murder. "A Rose for Emily" is the story of a *lady* and of her revenge for that grotesque identity.

"When Miss Emily Grierson died, our whole town went to her funeral." The public and communal nature of Emily's funeral, a festival that brings the town together, clarifying its social relationships and revitalizing its sense of the past, indicates her central role in Jefferson. Alive, Emily is town property and the subject of shared speculation; dead, she is town history and the subject of legend. It is her value as a symbol, however obscure and however ambivalent, of something that is of central significance to the identity of Jefferson and to the meaning of its history that compels the narrator to assume a communal voice to tell her story. For Emily, like Georgiana, is a man-made object, a cultural artifact, and what she is reflects and defines the culture that has produced her.

The history the narrator relates to us reveals Jefferson's continuous emotional involvement with Emily. Indeed, though she shuts herself up in a house which she rarely leaves and which no one enters, her furious isolation is in direct proportion to the town's obsession with her. Like Georgiana, she is the object of incessant attention; her every act is immediately consumed by the town for gossip and seized on to justify their interference in her affairs. Her private life becomes a public document that the town folk feel free to interpret at will, and they are alternately curious, jealous, spiteful, pitying, partisan, proud, disapproving, admiring, and vindicated. Her funeral is not simply a communal ceremony; it is also the climax of their invasion of her private life and the logical extension of their voyeuristic attitude toward her. Despite the narrator's demurral, getting inside Emily's house is the all-consuming desire of the town's population, both male and female; while the men may wait a little longer, their motive is still prurient curiosity: "Already we knew that there was one room in that region above stairs which no one had seen in forty years, and which would have to be forced. They waited until Miss Emily was decently in the ground before they opened it."

In a context in which the overtones of violation and invasion are so palpable, the word "decently" has that ironic ring which gives the game away. When the men finally do break down the door, they find that Emily has satisfied their prurience with a vengeance and in doing so has created for them a mirror image of themselves. The true nature of Emily's relation to Jefferson is contained in the analogies between what those who break open that room see in it and what has brought them there to see it. The perverse, violent, and grotesque aspects of the sight of Homer Barron's rotted corpse in a room decked out for a bridal and now faded and covered in dust reflects back to them the perverseness of their own prurient interest in Emily, the violence implicit in their continued invasions of her life, and the grotesqueness of the symbolic artifact they have made of her—their monument, their idol, their lady. Thus, the figure that Jefferson places at the center of its legendary history does indeed contain the clue to the meaning of that history—a history which began long before Emily's funeral and long before Homer Barron's disappearance or appearance and long before Colonel Sartoris' fathering of edicts and remittances. It is recorded in that emblem which lies at the heart of the town's memory and at the heart of patriarchal culture: "We had long thought of them as a tableau, Miss Emily a slender figure in white in the background, her father a spraddled silhouette in the foreground, his back to her and clutching a horsewhip, the two of them framed by the back-flung front door."

The importance of Emily's father in shaping the quality of her life is insistent throughout the story. Even in her death the force of his presence is felt; above her dead body sits "the crayon face of her father musing profoundly," symbolic of the degree to which he has dominated and shadowed her life, "as if that quality of her father which had thwarted her woman's life so many times had been too virulent and too furious to die." The violence of this consuming relationship is made explicit in the imagery of the tableau. Although the violence is apparently directed outward—the upraised horse-whip against the would-be suitor—the real object of it is the woman—daughter, forced into the background and dominated by the phallic figure of the spraddled father whose back is turned on her and who prevents her from getting out at the same time that he prevents them from getting in. Like Georgiana's spatial confinement in "The Birthmark," Emily's is a met-aphor for her psychic confinement: her identity is determined by the con-structs of her father's mind, and she can no more escape from his creation of her as "a slender figure in white" than she can escape his house.

What is true for Emily in relation to her father is equally true for her in relation to Jefferson: her status as a lady is a cage from which she cannot es-cape. To them she is always *Miss* Emily; she is never referred to and never thought of as otherwise. In omitting her title from his, Faulkner emphasizes the point that the real violence done to Emily is in making her a "Miss"; the omission is one of his roses for her. Because she is *Miss* Emily *Grierson*, Emily's father dresses her in white, places her in the background, and drives away her suitors. Because she is Miss Emily Grierson, the town invests her with that communal significance which makes her the object of their obses-sion and subject of their incessant scrutiny. And because she is a lady, the town is able to impose a particular code of behavior on her ("But there were still others, older people, who said that even grief could not cause a real lady to forget *noblesse oblige*") and to see in her failure to live up to that code an excuse for interfering in her life. As a lady, Emily is venerated, but venera-tion results in the more telling emotions of envy and spite; "It was another link between the gross, teeming world and the high and mighty Griersons"; "People . . . believed that the Griersons held themselves a little too high for what they really were." The violence implicit in the desire to see the monu-ment fall and reveal itself for clay suggests the violence inherent in the orig-inal impulse to venerate.

The violence behind veneration is emphasized through another telling emblem in the story. Emily's position as an hereditary obligation upon the town dates from "that day in 1894 when Colonel Sartoris, the mayor—he who fathered the edict that no Negro woman should appear on the streets without an apron on—remitted her taxes, the dispensation dating from the death of her father on into perpetuity." The conjunction of these two ac-tions in the same syntactic unit is crucial, for it insists on their essential sim-ilarity. It indicates that the impulse to exempt is analogous to the desire to restrict, and that what appears to be a kindness or an act of veneration is in fact an insult. Sartoris' remission of Emily's taxes is a public declaration of the fact that a lady is not considered to be, and hence not allowed or enabled to be, economically independent (consider, in this connection, Emily's lessons in china painting; they are a latter-day version of Sartoris' "charity" and a brilliant image of Emily's economic uselessness). His act is a public statement of the fact that a lady, if she is to survive, must have either husband or father, and that, because Emily has neither, the town must assume responsibility for her. The remission of taxes that defines Emily's status dates from the death of her father, and she is handed over from one patron to the next, the town instead of husband taking on the role of father. Indeed, the use of the word "fathered" in describing Sartoris' behavior as mayor underlines the fact that his chivalric attitude toward Emily is simply a subtler and more dishonest version of her father's horsewhip.

The narrator is the last of the patriarchs who take upon themselves the burden of defining Emily's life, and his violence toward her is the most subtle of all. His tone of incantatory reminiscence and nostalgic veneration seems free of the taint of horsewhip and edict. Yet a thoroughgoing contempt for the "ladies" who spy and pry and gossip out of their petty jealousy and curiosity is one of the clearest strands in the narrator's consciousness. Emily is exempted from the general indictment because she is a *real* lady— that is, eccentric, slightly crazy, obsolete, a "stubborn and coquettish decay," absurd but indulged; "dear, inescapable, impervious, tranquil, and perverse"; indeed, anything and everything but human.

Not only does "A Rose for Emily" expose the violence done to a woman by making her a lady; it also explores the particular form of power the victim gains from this position and can use on those who enact this violence. "A Rose for Emily" is concerned with the consequences of violence for both the violated and the violators. One of the most striking aspects of the story is the disparity between Miss Emily Grierson and the Emily to whom Faulkner gives his rose in ironic imitation of the chivalric behavior the story exposes. The form of Faulkner's title establishes a camaraderie between author and protagonist and signals that a distinction must be made between the story Faulkner is telling and the story the narrator is telling. This distinction is of major importance because it suggests, of course, that the narrator, looking through a patriarchal lens, does not see Emily at all but rather a figment of his own imagination created in conjunction with the cumulative imagination of the town. Like Ellison's invisible man, nobody sees *Emily.* And because nobody sees *her,* she can literally get away with murder. Emily is characterized by her ability to understand and utilize the power that accrues to her from the fact that men do not see her but rather their concept of her: "'I have no taxes in Jefferson. Colonel Sartoris explained it to me. . . . Tobe! . . . Show these gentlemen out.'" Relying on the conventional assumptions about ladies who are expected to be neither reasonable nor in touch with reality, Emily presents an impregnable front that vanquishes the men "horse and foot, just as she had vanquished their fathers thirty years before." In spite of their "modern" ideas, this new generation, when faced with Miss Emily, are as much bound by the code of gentlemanly behavior as their fathers were ("They rose when she entered"). This code gives Emily a power that renders the gentlemen unable to function in a situation in which a lady neither sits down herself nor asks them to. They are brought to a "stumbling halt" and can do nothing when confronted with her refusal to engage in rational discourse. Their only recourse in the face of such eccentricity is to engage in behavior unbecoming to gentlemen, and Emily can count on their continuing to see themselves as gentlemen and her as a lady and on their returning a verdict of helpless noninterference.

It is in relation to Emily's disposal of Homer Barron, however, that Faulkner demonstrates most clearly the power of conventional assumptions about the nature of ladies to blind the town to what is going on and to allow Emily to murder with impunity. When Emily buys the poison, it never occurs to anyone that she intends to use it on Homer, so strong is the presumption that ladies when jilted commit suicide, not murder. And when her house begins to smell, the women blame it on the eccentricity of having a man servant rather than a woman, "as if a man—any man—could keep a kitchen properly." And then they hint that her eccentricity may have shaded over into madness, "remembering how old lady Wyatt, her great aunt, had gone completely crazy at last." The presumption of madness, that preeminently female response to bereavement, can be used to explain away much in the behavior of ladies whose activities seem a bit odd.

But even more pointed is what happens when the men try not to explain but to do something about the smell: "'Dammit, sir,' Judge Stevens said, 'will you accuse a lady to her face of smelling bad?'" But if a lady cannot be told that she smells, then the cause of the smell cannot be discovered and so her crime is "perfect." Clearly, the assumptions behind the Judge's outraged retort go beyond the myth that ladies are out of touch with reality. His outburst insists that it is the responsibility of gentlemen to make them so. Ladies must not be confronted with facts; they must be shielded from all that is unpleasant. Thus Colonel Sartoris remits Emily's taxes with a palpably absurd story, designed to protect her from an awareness of her poverty and her dependence on charity, and to protect him from having to confront her with it. And thus Judge Stevens will not confront Emily with the fact that her house stinks, though she is living in it and can hardly be unaware of the odor. Committed as they are to the myth that ladies and bad smells cannot coexist, these gentlemen insulate themselves from reality. And by defining a lady as a subhuman and hence sublegal entity, they have created a situation their laws can't touch. They have made it possible for Emily to be extra-legal: "'Why, of course,' the druggist said, 'If that's what you want. But the law requires you to tell what you are going to use it for.' Miss Emily just stared at him, her head tilted back in order to look him eye for eye, until he looked away and went and got the arsenic and wrapped it up." And, finally, they have created a situation in which they become the criminals: "So the next night, after midnight, four men crossed Miss Emily's lawn and slunk about the house like burglars." Above them, "her upright torso motionless as that of an idol," sits Emily, observing them act out their charade of chivalry. As they leave, she confronts them with the reality they are trying to protect her from: she turns on the light so that they may see her watching them. One can only wonder at the fact, and regret, that she didn't call the sheriff and have them arrested for trespassing.

Not only is "A Rose for Emily" a supreme analysis of what men do to women by making them ladies; it is also an exposure of how this act in turn defines and recoils upon men. This is the significance of the dynamic that Faulkner establishes between Emily and Jefferson. And it is equally the point of the dynamic implied between the tableau of Emily and her father and the tableau which greets the men who break down the door of that room in the region above the stairs. When the would-be "suitors" finally get into her father's house, they discover the consequences of his oppression of her, for the violence contained in the rotted corpse of Homer Barron is the mirror image of the violence represented in the tableau, the back-flung front door flung back with a vengeance. Having been consumed by her father, Emily in turn feeds off Homer Barron, becoming, after his death, suspiciously fat. Or, to put it another way, it is as if, after her father's death, she has reversed his act of incorporating her by incorporating and becoming him, metamorphosed from the slender figure in white to the obese figure in black whose hair is "a vigorous iron-gray, like the hair of an active man." She has taken into herself the violence in him which thwarted her and has reenacted it upon Homer Barron.

That final encounter, however, is not simply an image of the reciprocity of violence. Its power of definition also derives from its grotesqueness, which makes finally explicit the grotesqueness that has been latent in the description of Emily throughout the story: "Her skeleton was small and spare; perhaps that was why what would have been merely plumpness in another was obesity in her. She looked bloated, like a body long submerged in motionless water, and of that pallid hue. Her eyes, lost in the fatty ridges of her face, looked like two small pieces of coal pressed into a lump of dough." The impact of this description depends on the contrast it establishes between Emily's reality as a fat, bloated figure in black and the conventional image of a lady—expectations that are fostered in the town by its emblematic memory of Emily as a slender figure in white and in us by the narrator's tone of romantic invocation and by the passage itself. Were she not expected to look so different, were her skeleton not small and spare, Emily would not be so grotesque. Thus, the focus is on the grotesqueness that results when stereotypes are imposed upon reality. And the implication of this focus is that the real grotesque is the stereotype itself. If Emily is both lady and grotesque, then the syllogism must be completed thus: the idea of a lady is grotesque. So Emily is metaphor and mirror for the town of Jefferson; and when, at the end, the town folk finally discover who and what she is, they have in fact encountered who and what they are.

Despite similarities of focus and vision, "A Rose for Emily" is more implicitly feminist than "The Birthmark." For one thing, Faulkner does not have Hawthorne's compulsive ambivalence; one is not invited to misread "A Rose for Emily" as one is invited to misread "The Birthmark." Thus the interpretation of "The Birthmark" that sees it as a story of misguided idealism, despite its massive oversights, nevertheless *works;* while the efforts to read "A Rose for Emily" as a parable of the relations between North and South, or as a conflict between an old order and a new, or as a story about the human relation to Time, don't work because the attempt to make Emily representative of such concepts stumbles over the fact that woman's condition is not the "human" condition. To understand Emily's experience requires a primary awareness of the fact that she is a woman.

But, more important, Faulkner provides us with an image of retaliation. Unlike Georgiana, Emily does not simply acquiesce; she prefers to murder rather than to die. In this respect she is a welcome change from the image of woman as willing victim that fills the pages of our literature, and whose other face is the ineffective fulminations of Dame Van Winkle. Nevertheless, Emily's action is still reaction. "A Rose for Emily" exposes the poverty of a situation in which turnabout is the only possibility and in which one's acts are neither self-generated nor self-determined but are simply a response to and a reflection of forces outside oneself. Though Emily may be proud, strong, and indomitable, her murder of Homer Barron is finally an indication of the severely limited nature of the power women can wrest from the system that oppresses them. Aylmer's murder of Georgiana is an indication of men's absolute power over women; it is an act performed in the complete security of his ability to legitimize it as a noble and human pursuit. Emily's act has no such context. It is possible only because it can be kept secret; and it can be kept secret only at the cost of exploiting her image as a lady. Furthermore, Aylmer murders Georgiana in order to get rid of her; Emily murders Homer Barron in order to have him.

Patriarchal culture is based to a considerable extent on the argument that men and women are made for each other and on the conviction that "masculinity" and "femininity" are the natural reflection of that divinely ordained complement. Yet, if one reads "The Birthmark" and "A Rose for Emily" as analyses of the consequences of a massive differentiation of everything according to sex, one sees that in reality a sexist culture is one in which men and women are not simply incompatible but murderously so. Aylmer murders Georgianna because he must at any cost get rid of woman; Emily murders Homer Barron because she must at any cost get a man. The two stories define the disparity between cultural myth and cultural reality, and they suggest that in this disparity is the ultimate grotesque.

GENE M. MOORE

Of Time and Its Mathematical Progression: Problems of Chronology in Faulkner's "A Rose for Emily"

Over the past 30 years, no fewer than *eight* different chronologies have been proposed to account for the events occurring in William Faulkner's celebrated short story "A Rose for Emily."[1] These chronologies cover a span of 14 years (Miss Emily was born between 1850 and 1864, and died between 1924 and 1938), and they make use of many different kinds of evidence: not only internal temporal references and cross-references in the story, but also historical, biographical, canonical, and even forensic evidence. Given the amount of interest generated by this question and the range of evidence employed in the various arguments, it is remarkable that no one seems ever to have regarded the original manuscript as a possible source of chronological information; in fact, evidence from the manuscript makes it possible to solve some of the problems of Miss Emily's chronology by fixing the date of her father's death.

While critics have recognized the importance of time to a proper understanding of the story—in the words of Ray B. West, Jr., "The subject of the story is man's relation to Time" (Inge 36)—they have also complained, in strong and vivid language, of the difficulty of establishing a consistent chronology: "Faulkner destroys chronological time in his story" (Magalaner and Volpe, cited in Inge 63); he uses "a complicatedly disjunctive time scheme" (Wilson 56) that "twists chronology almost beyond recognition" (Sullivan 167); his technique is an "abandonment of chronology" (A. M. Wright, cited in Sullivan 167). Yet whether the story of Miss Emily Grierson is to be understood in terms of conflict between the North and the South, between the Old South and the New South, or between the "past" and the "present," for the sake of all these arguments it is vitally important to establish her own chronological place in the historical context of the passing generations. What dates are carved on Miss Emily's tombstone?

The task at hand has never been stated more simply than by William T. Going in the earliest of the chronologies: "By means of internal or external evidence, date the major events of Emily Grierson's life" (8). Yet in practice it is often difficult to distinguish "internal" from "external" evidence. Is evidence from the unrevised manuscript of "A Rose for Emily" internal or external? What about references to Judge Stevens or Colonel Sartoris in other works by Faulkner? In general, what constitutes legitimate chronological evidence? In cases of conflict, what forms of evidence should take precedence over others? The "internal" chronology of a given work may or may not prove to be consistent, and may or may not be attached (consistently or inconsistently) to a variety of "external" chronologies based on information such as references occurring in other works by the same author (*canonical* evidence), or what we know about the author's life (*biographical* evidence) or the context of history in general (*historical* evidence). In each case, specific chronological references can be either *absolute*, in the form of dates (such as the single reference to 1894 in "A Rose for Emily"); *relative* to other references (e.g., "the summer after her father's death," "thirty years before"); or *contextual*, establishing a measure of time with reference to historical or natural codes of temporality outside the text (e.g., allusions to the Civil War signify 1861–65; the graying of Miss Emily's hair is a gradual process; dead bodies decompose at a certain rate under certain conditions, etc.). The discrepancies among the eight chronologies are largely a result of underlying differences of opinion about the relative weights to be accorded these various kinds of evidence.

The specific difficulty of establishing a chronology for Miss Emily arises largely because the first half of her story is told essentially in reverse chronological order, and the events in it are described not in terms of dates or specific historical references, but most often in terms of her age at the time. Anchoring this "internal" chronology in history requires, in effect, that we find at least one point of attachment between "internal" references to Miss Emily's age or activities, and "external" references to dates or known historical events.

Most of the discussion in the eight chronologies has centered upon two problematic events in her life: the remission of her taxes by Colonel Sartoris in 1894, and the period of china-painting lessons "when she was about forty." 1894 is the only date mentioned in the story, but its exact position in Miss Emily's life (i.e., her age at the time) is by no means certain. In the third paragraph of the story, reference is made to "that day in 1894 when Colonel Sartoris, the mayor . . . remitted her taxes, the dispensation dating from the death of her father on into perpetuity." This means, at the least, that her father died no later than 1894. We are told that at the time of her father's death Miss Emily had "got to be thirty and was still single"; and when she buys the poison about two years later, the narrator reminds us that "She was over thirty then." The year 1864 is thus a *terminus ad quem* for Miss Emily's birth, and is respected as such by all the chronologists.

Some, however, have taken 1894 as the point of attachment between Emily's life and historical chronology, assuming that her taxes were remitted immediately following her father's death, and that he accordingly died that same year (McGlynn, Wilson). Her age at the time is taken as 30 (McGlynn) or 32 (Wilson), indicating that she was born in 1862 or 1864 and died in 1936 or 1938. However, "A Rose for Emily" was first published in 1930, creating a "glaring discrepancy" that led Helen E. Nebeker to revise her original chronology ("Chronology Revised" 471), and that in Menakhem Perry's opinion leads to "absurd conclusions" (344n26). Nebeker and Perry take 1930, the date of publication, as a *terminus ad quem* for Miss Emily's death, which means that the year 1856 becomes the corresponding *terminus* for her birth.[2]

The remission of Miss Emily's taxes is mentioned twice in the story: first as occurring in 1894, and second in connection with the period of her china-painting lessons "when she was about forty": the narrator ends the paragraph describing these lessons with the remark that "Meanwhile her taxes had been remitted." Some chronologists have taken this "Meanwhile" to mean that Miss Emily must have been "about forty" in 1894, and that she was therefore born in 1854 and died in 1928 (Hagopian et al., Nebeker, "Emily's Rose . . . : A Postscript" and "Chronology Revised"). Brooks's chronology is a numerical compromise between those of Going and Hagopian et al., according to which Miss Emily, born in 1852, would have been 42 in 1894. Perry also takes this "Meanwhile" as indicative of simultaneity: "She was exempted from taxation in the period when she gave chinapainting lessons" (344n26). In other words, much of the discrepancy among the various chronologies can be understood as a result of the choice of where to attach the historical "anchor" of the remission of taxes in 1894: to the death of Miss Emily's father when she was "over thirty," or to the chinapainting period when she was "about forty"?

Surprisingly, what no one seems to have noticed or taken seriously is that in the original manuscript Faulkner assigned a different date to the remission of Miss Emily's taxes and a specific date to her father's death: the corresponding passage in the manuscript speaks of "that day in 1904 when Colonel Sartoris . . . remitted her taxes dating from the death of her father 16 years back, on into perpetuity" (Inge 8).[3] One can only speculate about why Faulkner found it necessary to shift the date of Colonel Sartoris' gallant action back ten years from 1904 to 1894, and to delete all reference to the "16 years" since the father's death. Perhaps 16 years seemed too long for Miss Emily to remain actively on the minds of city officials? In any event, it is clear that when Faulkner originally committed the story to paper, her taxes were remitted not in 1894 but in 1904, 16 years after the death of her father in 1888. Restoring Faulkner's alterations and deletions may seem to run counter to the editorial principle of respecting the author's final intentions; but keeping the original dates in mind can help untangle the story's chronology.

The altered date and the omission of the reference to "16 years back" in the typescript version need not mean that Faulkner had necessarily changed his mind about the date of Miss Emily's father's death. Had he moved it back the same 10 years, she would have to have been born before 1848 to have been over 30 by 1878, and would thus have been of the same generation as the Civil War veterans who attend her funeral. As Brooks noted,

The "very old men—some in their brushed Confederate uniforms" who, at the funeral, talked "of Miss Emily as if she had been a contemporary of theirs, believing that they had danced with her and courted her" must have been a number of years older than she. (*WF: Toward Yoknapatawpha and Beyond* 383)[4]

However, in the earliest of the chronologies, William T. Going invoked Faulkner's authority to the effect that Miss Emily was born in 1850 and died in 1924, since 1924 was the date assigned to "A Rose for Emily" in Malcolm Cowley's Viking Portable edition of Faulkner's works (1946), in which Cowley noted editorially that dates were assigned "with the author's consent and later with his advice at doubtful points" (cited in Inge 51).[5] Going set the date of her father's death as early as 1882.

Manuscript evidence cannot solve all the chronological problems, since the china-painting period is defined not only in connection with Miss Emily's being "about forty," but also retrospectively, working backward from later events: the death of Colonel Sartoris, the visit of the tax delegation, and her own death. We are told that no one had seen the house's interior for "at least ten years" before she died, and that the visit of the tax delegation (which may or may not have been the last visit before her death, but is in any case the only visit we are told about) took place "eight or ten years" after she ceased giving china-painting lessons and "almost ten years" after the death of Colonel Sartoris.[6] In other words, she died at least 18 years after the last lessons were given: 18 years before her death at age 74, Miss Emily would have been 56 years old, so that if the lessons lasted for "a period of six or seven years," Miss Emily could not have been "about forty" at the time, but would instead have been about 50. Paul D. McGlynn has attempted to disregard this problem by suggesting that "Of course 'about forty' might well be a genteel euphemism for 'about fifty'" (Inge 91; cf. Wilson 59); but this suggestion still does not explain why the narrator would protect Miss Emily's age only at this particular point and not elsewhere. Would anyone wish to read the narrator's two references to her being "over thirty" as genteel euphemisms for "over forty," or the announcement of her "death at seventy-four" as a coded euphemism for 84? In effect, the chronology to be established by tracing the course of Miss Emily's life forward from the time of her father's death fails to square with the chronology to be derived retrospectively from the time of her own death.

Interpreting the reference to "at least ten years" as possibly allowing for as much as 20 years is also no solution, since the visit of the tax delegation is the peg from which the date of the smell "thirty years before" is hung. Internal references indicate that Homer Barron must have died when Miss Emily was about 33 or 34 years old: at least 40 years before her own death (equal to the "at least ten years" since the last visit plus the 30 years since the smell), and two years after her father's death, which occurred when she was already at least 30.[7] A limit is thereby set to the range of time included in "at least": her last visit had to occur "at least ten years" and at most 12 years before her death, since if it occurred more than 12 years earlier, she would have been under 30 when her father died.

In summary, the chronologies can be divided roughly into two groups: one group—Woodward, McGlynn, Nebeker ("Emily's Rose . . . : Thematic Implications"), and Wilson—connects the tax remission of 1894 with her father's death (Emily is between 30 and 34 in 1894); while the other— Going, Hagopian et al., Nebeker ("Emily's Rose . . . : A Postscript" and "Chronology Revised"), Brooks, and Perry—links the reference to 1894 with the period of china-painting (i.e., Emily is "about forty," or between 39 and 42, in 1894). The first group tends to disregard the narrator's reference to the remission of taxes as being retroactive: "the dispensation dating from the death of her father on into perpetuity." Taxes are collected annually—"On the first of the year they mailed her a tax notice"—so that if Miss Emily's taxes were remitted the same year her father died, the narrator's reference to the retroactive nature of the remission would appear to be unnecessary.

This much can be determined on the basis of "internal" references alone; but the references to Colonel Sartoris and to Judge Stevens lead us outside the story to look for external canonical evidence in the form of references to these gentlemen in other works by Faulkner. If Judge Stevens was already 80 years old and mayor at the time of the smell (which the chronologies date variously between 1884 and 1896), then he is probably too old to be Judge Lemuel Stevens, the father of Gavin Stevens, who is mentioned in Faulkner's late works: he would have been between 102 and 114 years old at the time of his death in 1918—perhaps not an altogether impossible age, but one remarkable enough to be worth mentioning. Nevertheless, most of the glossaries and indexes have identified the elderly Judge Stevens of "A Rose for Emily" with Judge Lemuel (Brooks, *WF: The Yoknapatawpha Country* 483; Ford and Kincaid 96; Kirk and Klotz 349); only Runyan has created a separate entry for the Judge Stevens of "A Rose for Emily" (158).

Similar problems arise with the reference to a Colonel Sartoris who was mayor in 1894 and who died "almost ten years" before the visit of the tax delegation (and thus about 20 years before Miss Emily's death, when she was about 54). Once again, there is some doubt about which Colonel Satoris is meant: Faulkner has described the early history of the Sartoris family more thoroughly than that of the Stevenses, so that it appears correspondingly more difficult to imagine a strange new Colonel Sartoris, unique to "A Rose for Emily" and unmentioned elsewhere, who could have been mayor in 1894. Faulkner's works mention two Colonel Sartorises: Colonel John

Sartoris, who dies too early to have been Miss Emily's mayor in 1894, and his son Bayard—"the banker with his courtesy title acquired partly by inheritance and partly by propinquity" (*Reivers* 74)—who dies too late. The death of the original Colonel John Sartoris at the hands of his partner Ben J. Redmond (a.k.a. Redlaw) is given three different dates in three other works, all of them well before 1894: 1874 in *The Unvanquished;* "Aug. 4, 1876" in *Flags in the Dust* (428); and 1878 in *Requiem for a Nun* (205). This Colonel's son (the young Bayard of *The Unvanquished*) first appears in Faulkner's works as the Old Bayard of *Flags in the Dust,* where his death is clearly described as having occurred in December 1919 (351)—too late to correspond to the story of Miss Emily.[8] Predictably, the indexes and glossaries are split on this issue: forced to make a choice, some identify Miss Emily's Sartoris with Colonel John (Brooks, *WF: The Yoknapatawpha Country* 480), while others match him with Colonel Bayard (Ford and Kincaid 85, Kirk and Klotz 346, Runyan 142).

However, the original date of 1904 for the mayoral edict may help to solve this problem as well, since young Bayard Sartoris could well have been mayor at that time. We are told in *The Reivers* of his propensity for passing edicts, although he is not specifically named as mayor; when his matched carriage horses are startled by a home-made automobile, "by the next night there was formally recorded into the archives of Jefferson a city ordinance against the operation of any mechanically propelled vehicle inside the corporate limits" (27–28); additional information in *The Reivers* makes it possible to date this incident as having occurred in 1904. The Colonel's tendency to govern by radical edict is mentioned in "A Rose for Emily" as well, since it was "he who fathered the edict that no Negro woman should appear on the streets without an apron" (119–20).

In conclusion, the neglected manuscript evidence, by allowing us to fix the date of the death of Miss Emily's father in 1888, makes it possible to establish a chronology that is different from the eight that have been suggested previously (although it differs from that of Perry by only one year). Perhaps when Faulkner decided to move the time of Miss Emily's tax remission back by ten years, he simply failed to consider the consequences of this alteration for the rest of the chronology. Yet whether the year in question is 1894 or 1904, the internal inconsistency of the period of her china-painting remains, together with the canonical inconsistencies concerning the identities of Judge Stevens and Colonal Sartoris. The ancient Civil War veterans who try to remember Miss Emily are not alone in having to cope with the problem of "confusing time with its mathematical progression."

APPENDIX: A CHRONOLOGY
FOR MISS EMILY GRIERSON

1856: Miss Emily is born; the narrator never mentions her birth directly, but his reference to "the day of her death at seventy-four" defines the parameters of any chronology in terms of a span of 74 years.

1870–1879: The Grierson house is built "in the heavily lightsome style of the seventies," thus presumably during the 1870s.

1888: Her father dies after "she got to be thirty."

1889: She meets Homer Barron "the summer after her father's death."

1890: She buys arsenic from the druggist "over a year after they had begun to say 'Poor Emily'. . . . She was over thirty then." She poisons Homer Barron, who disappears "two years after her father's death"; a smell is noticed "a short time after," which is also "thirty years before" the tax visit.

1893–1900: Miss Emily is "about forty"; she gives lessons in china-painting "for a period of six or seven years."

1894: "Meanwhile" Colonel Sartoris, the mayor, remits her taxes.

1920: She is visited by a deputation of the Board of Aldermen "eight or ten years" after she stops giving china-painting lessons and "almost ten years" after the death of Colonel Sartoris.

1930: She dies "at least ten years" since her last visit, presumably from the tax deputation; after her funeral, the room, "which no one has seen in forty years," is opened.

WORKS CITED

Brooks, Cleanth. *William Faulkner: The Yoknapatawpha Country*. New Haven: Yale UP, 1963.

———. *William Faulkner: Toward Yoknapatawpha and Beyond*. New Haven: Yale UP, 1978.

Cowley, Malcolm. Introduction. *The Portable Faulkner*. New York: Viking, 1946. 1–24.

Cullen, John B., and Floyd C. Watkins. "Miss Emily." *Old Times in the Faulkner Country*. Chapel Hill: U of North Carolina P, 1961. 70–71. Rpt. in Inge 17–18.

Faulkner, William. *Collected Stories of William Faulkner*. New York: Random, 1950.

———. *Flags in the Dust*. New York: Random, 1973.

———. *Requiem for a Nun*. New York: Random, 1950.

———. *The Reivers*. New York: Random, 1962.

———. "A Rose for Emily." *Collected Stories* 119–30.

———. *The Unvanquished.* New York: Random, 1938.

———. *William Faulkner Manuscripts: These 13.* Ed. Noel Polk. New York: Garland, 1985. 188–214.

Ford, Margaret Patricia, and Suzanne Kincaid. *Who's Who in Faulkner.* N.p.: Louisiana State UP, 1963.

Genette, Gérard. *Narrative Discourse: An Essay in Method.* Trans. Jane E. Lewin. Ithaca: Cornell UP, 1980.

Going, William T. "Chronology in Teaching 'A Rose for Emily.'" *Exercise Exchange* 5 (February 1958): 8–11. Rpt. in Inge 50–53.

Hagopian, John V., W. Gordon Cunliffe, and Martin Dolch. "A Rose for Emily," *Insight I: Analyses of American Literature.* Frankfurt: Hirschgraben, 1964. 43–50. Rpt. in Inge 76–83.

Inge, M. Thomas, ed. *William Faulkner: A Rose for Emily.* The Charles E. Merrill Literary Casebook Series. Columbus, OH: Merrill, 1970.

Kirk, Robert W., and Marvin Klotz. *Faulkner's People: A Complete Guide and Index to Characters in the Fiction of William Faulkner.* Berkeley: U of California P, 1963.

McGlynn, Paul D. "The Chronology of 'A Rose for Emily.'" *Studies in Short Fiction* 6 (1969): 461–62. Rpt. in Inge 90–92.

Nebeker, Helen E. "Emily's Rose of Love: Thematic Implications of Point of View in Faulkner's 'A Rose for Emily.'" *Bulletin of the Rocky Mountain Modern Language Association* 24 (1970): 3–13.

———. "Emily's Rose of Love: A Postscript." *Bulletin of the Rocky Mountain Modern Language Association* 24 (1970): 190–91.

———. "Chronology Revised." *Studies in Short Fiction* 8 (1971): 471–73.

Perry, Menakhem. "Literary Dynamics: How the Order of a Text Creates its Meanings [With an Analysis of Faulkner's 'A Rose for Emily']." *Poetics Today* 1:1–2 (Autumn 1979): 35–64, 311–61.

Runyan, Harry. *A Faulkner Glossary.* New York: Citadel, 1964.

Sullivan, Ruth. "The Narrator in 'A Rose for Emily.'" *Journal of Narrative Technique* 1 (1971): 159–78.

Wilson, G. R., Jr. "The Chronology of Faulkner's 'A Rose for Emily' Again." *Notes on Mississippi Writers* 5 (Fall 1972): 56, 44, 58–62.

Woodward, Robert H. "The Chronology of 'A Rose for Emily.'" *Exercise Exchange* 8 (March 1966): 17–19. Rpt. in Inge 84–86.

NOTES

1 These chronologies were proposed by—in chronological order—Going (1958), Hagopian et al. (1964), Woodward (1966), McGlynn (1969), Nebeker (1970 and 1971), Wilson (1972), Brooks (1978), and Perry (1979). The first four were reprinted in Inge's 1970 casebook. Cleanth Brooks refers to five chronologies in this casebook (382n), but I have only been able to discover four, and my count is confirmed by the list in one of the suggestions

for short papers at the end of Inge's volume (127). Helen E. Nebeker has proposed two different chronologies (the first is "Emily's Rose . . . : Thematic Implications" and the second in "Emily's Rose: A Postscript" and "Chronology Revised"). Although different evidence is used, Nebeker's second chronology agrees with that proposed by Hagopian et al.

² The provisional futurism of a situation in which Miss Emily dies fictionally some years after the announcement of her death in the "real" world, as posited in half of the published chronologies (those of Woodward, McGlynn, Nebeker ["Emily's Rose . . . : Thematic Implications"], and Wilson), is not without literary precedent: Gérard Genette has noted a similar discrepancy in the case of Proust's *A la recherche du temps perdu*, where the final scenes are required by internal chronology to take place "about 1925," some three years after the death of Marcel Proust (Genette 91ff.). Genette remarks that this discrepancy is "an inconvenience only if one claims to identify the hero with the author" (91n11). In the case of "A Rose for Emily," the "inconvenience" indeed exists only if one claims to identify the fictional world of Miss Emily with the historical world of William Faulkner; but this claim is at the origin of any attempt to set up a chronology.

³ This oversight is all the more remarkable in view of the fact that a quite legible reproduction of the first manuscript page was printed as an illustration in Inge's 1970 casebook, which all the later critics have cited as a reference.

⁴ On similar historical grounds, one could argue that the Homer Barron episode must be set much later, since the actual streets of Oxford were not paved until the 1920s (Cullen and Watkins 71, cited in Inge 17).

⁵ Cowley also acknowledged in his Introduction that "As one book leads into another, Faulkner sometimes falls into inconsistencies of detail." He added that "these errors are comparatively few and inconsequential. . . . I should judge that most of them are afterthoughts rather than oversights" (Cowley 7–8).

⁶ In the place of the reference to the china-painting lessons as having ceased "eight or ten years earlier," the unrevised manuscript reads "6 or 7 years ago" (Faulkner, *Manuscripts* 189).

⁷ G. R. Wilson, Jr. has confirmed this part of the chronology on the canonical grounds that 33, Miss Emily's age when she begins riding out with Homer Barron, is "Faulkner's favorite age for bringing his central figures to their point of crisis" (58). Joe Christmas indeed comes to grief at age 33, but this favoritism does not seem to apply to the Sartorises, Bundrens, Compsons, Sutpens, McCaslins, or Beauchampses who are the central figures of his other novels and stories.

⁸ The date of Old Bayard's death is irrevocably fixed as post–First World War, since he dies in the company of his grandson and namesake, who has returned from the war in France. Going has taken the reference to the death of Colonel John Sartoris in *Requiem for a Nun* (205) as indicating twelve years after 1876 (Inge 51); but the same passage can be read as 1876 plus only two years, depending on whether one regards the material in parentheses as coming after the introductory reference to "another ten years," as Going does, or during the ten years in question, as I prefer to do.

Sample Student Research Paper

Schmidt 1

Meredith Schmidt

Professor Polk

English 201

April 17, 2000

The Teller of the Tale

William Faulkner's "A Rose for Emily" is told by
a first-person narrator who speaks as the voice Introduction
of the town of Jefferson, or at least as their
repository of information about Emily Grierson.
Emily's life and death are clearly the object of
much speculation, concern, titillation, and rumor for several generations of Jeffersonians, including the narrator. The narrator does not tell
us much about himself or herself. We do not even
know the narrator's age, gender, or race, though
we may presume he or she is a white person if
only because the narrator is among those, also
presumably white, who after Emily's funeral break
down the locked door to the room where Emily has
kept Homer Barron's body. Sometimes the narrator
positions himself outside the community, as an
observer, and the narration turns to third person: "They just said, 'Poor Emily'" (Polk 19;
emphasis added). On other occasions, the narrator
seems to merge into the larger community, as participant, and so uses the first-person plural pronoun to narrate: "When we saw her again . . ."

Schmidt 2

(18); "the next day <u>we</u> all said . . ." (20); "<u>we</u> were not surprised" (20; emphasis added).

This narrator seems to be describing the town's relations with Emily, although many scholars (Sullivan, for example) argue that he (Sullivan assumes a male) is intimately involved in the story he is telling in ways he is not completely honest about. Terry Heller would seem to agree: "[. . .] the narrator fails to give us pertinent information we assume that he has: he must know in what order Emily bought the toilet articles, the clothing, and the poison" (Polk, 41). It is also possible, as Heller suggests, that the narrator does not understand everything: "The narrator appears also to be rather uncertain about Emily's true character" (42–43). Even though he does assume some authoritative control over the narrative of Emily's life, this narrator, unlike an omniscient narrator, does not claim to know everything, and in fact, the narrator tells this story as much through what he does not know as through what he does know. Part of the eerie power of the story's final scene comes from readers' realization that we, finally, help to create Miss Emily's story out of the bits and pieces the narrator gives us from the town's collective memory.

There seems to be no doubt, for example, that Miss Emily has killed Homer Barron with

Thesis statement

What the narrator does not know

Schmidt 3

the arsenic she has bought from the pharmacist in town, or that she lay with Barron at least once before locking the room and, apparently, never returning to it. That is, we believe what the narrator claims to have seen in this final scene. On several occasions, however, the narrator reports as truth things that he or she does not claim to witness. For example, the narrator is not likely to have been present when Miss Emily bought the arsenic at the drugstore (19-20), but reports the incident in considerable detail, even quoting their conversation. Likewise, the narrator reports in considerable detail the scene of the Board of Aldermen's visit to Miss Emily to try to force her to pay her taxes, describing, for example, how the house's front hall "smelled of dust and disuse--a close, dank smell" (16) and how Miss Emily herself looked "bloated, like a body long submerged in motionless water, and of that pallid hue" (16). These are details that only one present at the scene could have noticed, yet the narrator gives no indication of being present and indeed narrates the scene not with "we" but with "they."

Furthermore, it is clear that at least some of what the narrator claims "we"--the town--knew is suspect because it is based in rumor and innuendo. For example, after reporting that "<u>a neighbor</u> saw the Negro man admit [Homer Barron] at [Miss Emily's] kitchen door at dusk one evening,"

Schmidt 4

the narrator then says, "that was the last <u>we</u> saw of Homer Barron" (21; emphasis added); it never seems to occur to the narrator to question the accuracy of this neighbor's eyesight at dusk and so, like the community, takes the single vision as the truth.

The question for readers is this: Why does Faulkner employ a first-person narrator for this story in the first place, instead of an omniscient narrator, one who would know everything and could therefore be trusted to tell the complete truth about every incident? Perhaps he does so in order to allow readers to participate in shaping the story.

The narrator, however, does not claim to know everything and, as noted, builds the story out of much speculation about Emily. The narrator represents the town's collective interest and emotional investment in Miss Emily's life. Isaac Rodman argues that "The narrative weave contains two voices, that of a surface narrator who accurately portrays the voice of the town, and that of a deeper narrator who conceals his judgments but allows his tone to indicate his perspective [. . .]" (Polk, 83). But it seems clear that Faulkner uses his narrator precisely to give a single voice to the town's multiple, fragmented, complicated, and often contradictory narrative about Miss Emily. For them she is equally "dear, inescapable, impervious, tranquil,

How other critics view the narrator

Schmidt 5

and perverse" (21) all at the same time. They
want to control her sexual life as her father
had (they call in the aunts from Alabama and the
Baptist preacher to help), and yet take an interest in her courtship by Homer Barron, being
alternately glad that she finally has a love interest and falsely sympathetic. "Poor Emily,"
they say (19)--to think that one of the high
and mighty Griersons would have fallen so low
as to "'think seriously of a Northerner, a day
laborer'" (19). They are both nosy and judgmen-
tal, patronizing and caring, dominant and subordinate. They think they know her because they
have watched her for years and because they think
they "know" a "Southern woman." But they do not
know her very well at all. What they perceive
in her as independence and arrogance is, in sad
fact, something quite different.

The narrator's partial knowledge of Emily
thus reflects the community's partial knowledge.
In addition, Faulkner uses the gaps in the narrator's and the community's knowledge to draw
the reader into his story in ways that make it
necessary for the reader to participate in the
narrative itself, especially in the final scene.
The scene shocks the reader with its sudden and
dramatic revelation of Emily's perversion, a revelation that the narrator, building on partial
knowledge, has carefully prepared us for. Although apparently merely describing the scene, not
explaining it, the narrator has very carefully

Schmidt 6

crafted the narrative to lead us to fairly inescapable conclusions: that Emily murdered Homer
with the arsenic; that it was his rotting body
that created the odor emanating from under her
house; and that the narrator's dramatic emphasis,
in the closing line, on the telltale iron-gray
strand of hair lying beside the corpse, clearly
indicates that something perverse has taken place
here. Readers noting the various portraits of her
father as a dominating presence in her life--he
"thwarted her woman's life," the narrator tells
us (21)--automatically see in her liaison with
and murder of Homer both a rebellion against her
father and a very interesting Oedipal relationship with her father (Scherting), which only adds
to the sense of sexual and psychological perversion in the story.

However, the story provides no evidence to
prove that Emily murdered Homer; she bought the
arsenic, but no one else sees her give it to
him. Nor is it completely clear that his rotting
body provided the odor that disturbed the neighbors. Finally, the story provides no evidence
of any sort of sexual relationship between Emily
and Homer. Although the narrator's emphasis on
the sexually perverse in the final scene provides
a dramatic conclusion to the story, other possible narratives could have led to the scene in
the locked room. Perhaps he died from arsenic,
perhaps from natural causes; perhaps they lay
together once, perhaps many times over years.

Possibilities that
Faulkner's narrator
does not propose

Schmidt 7

Clearly she has not lain with the corpse for years prior to her death, since there is so much undisturbed dust on the bed and in the room. What if what she wanted, and got, from Homer was not a passionate sex life but merely the touch of another human being, the sort of touch her father had denied her? How infinitely more touching, how infinitely sadder, to understand that what the community and the narrator see as arrogance and defiance is no more than a broken heart that wanted love it could not have, that feared exposure and shame.

What is important here is not necessarily to deny that Miss Emily murdered Homer or to deny the sexual, Oedipal implications of her relationship with her father, but rather to suggest that the brilliance of Faulkner's choice of a narrator for this story lies in the multiplicity of stories that his narrative allows and even encourages. An omniscient narrator would have supplied all the answers. This narrator, if we read carefully, mostly supplies questions about Miss Emily's life, questions that we as readers are invited to answer in our own voices, in our own ways. We thus become narrators of this story, too--participants in the community of narrative that is Faulkner's Jefferson. Who, then, is the teller of this tale? In a sense, we readers are.

Conclusion: Who is the real narrator?

Works Cited

Heller, Terry. "The Telltale Hair: A Critical
    Study of William Faulkner's 'A Rose for
    Emily.'" Polk, 33–47.

Polk, Noel, ed. <u>William Faulkner's "A Rose for
    Emily."</u> The Harcourt Casebook Series in Lit-
    erature. Fort Worth: Harcourt, 2000.

Rodman, Isaac. "Irony and Isolation: Narrative
    Distance in Faulkner's 'A Rose for Emily.'"
    Polk, 82–91.

Scherting, Jack. "Emily Grierson's Oedipus Com-
    plex: Motif, Motive, and Meaning in Faulk-
    ner's 'A Rose for Emily.'" Polk, 110–119.

Sullivan, Ruth. "The Narrator in 'A Rose for
    Emily.'" Polk, 62–82.

Bibliography

Works by William Faulkner

NOVELS

Soldiers' Pay. New York: Boni, 1926.
Mosquitoes. New York: Boni, 1927.
Sartoris. New York: Harcourt, 1929.
The Sound and the Fury. New York: Cape, 1929.
As I Lay Dying. New York: Cape, 1930.
Sanctuary. New York: Cape, 1931.
Light in August. New York: Smith, 1932.
Pylon. New York: Smith,1935.
Absalom, Absalom! New York: Random, 1936.
The Unvanquished. New York: Random, 1938.
The Wild Palms. New York: Random, 1939.
The Hamlet. New York: Random,1940.
Go Down, Moses. New York: Random, 1942.
Intruder in the Dust. New York: Random, 1948.
Requiem for a Nun. New York: Random, 1951.
A Fable. New York: Random, 1954.
The Town. New York: Random, 1957.
The Mansion. New York: Random, 1959.
The Reivers. New York: Random, 1962.

STORIES

These 13. New York: Cape, 1931.
Idyll in the Desert. New York: Random, 1931.
Miss Zilphia Gant. Dallas: Book Club of Texas, 1932.
Dr. Martino. New York: Cape, 1934.
Knight's Gambit. New York: Random, 1949.
Collected Stories. New York: Random, 1950.
Big Woods. New York: Random, 1955.
Uncollected Stories. Ed. Joseph L. Blotner. New York: Random, 1977.

148

POEMS

The Marble Faun. New York: Four Seas, 1924.
A Green Bough. New York: Smith, 1933.

NONFICTION PROSE

Essays Speeches & Public Letters. Ed. James B. Meriwether. New York: Random, 1966.

INTERVIEWS

Faulkner in the University. Ed. Frederick L. Gwynn and Joseph L. Blotner. New York: Random, 1959.
Lion in the Garden: Interviews with William Faulkner, 1926–1962. Ed. James B. Meriwether and Michael Millgate. New York: Random, 1968.

LETTERS

Selected Letters of William Faulkner. Ed. Joseph L. Blotner. New York: Random, 1977.
Thinking of Home. Ed. James G. Watson. New York: Norton, 1992.

COLLECTIONS

William Faulkner: Novels 1930–1935. Ed. Joseph L. Blotner and Noel Polk. New York: Library of America, 1985. Contains *As I Lay Dying, Sanctuary, Light in August,* and *Pylon.*
William Faulkner: Novels 1936–1940. Ed. Joseph L. Blotner and Noel Polk. New York: Library of America, 1990. Contains *Absalom, Absalom!, The Unvanquished, If I Forget Thee, Jerusalem [The Wild Palms],* and *The Hamlet.*
William Faulkner: Novels 1942–1954. Ed. Joseph L. Blotner and Noel Polk. New York: Library of America, 1994. Contains *Go Down, Moses, Intruder in the Dust, Requiem for a Nun,* and *A Fable.*
William Faulkner: Novels 1957–1962. Ed. Joseph L. Blotner and Noel Polk. New York: Library of America, 1999. Contains *The Town, The Mansion,* and *The Reivers.*

Works about William Faulkner

BIOGRAPHIES

Blotner, Joseph L. *Faulkner: A Biography.* 2 vols. New York: Random, 1974. Rev. ed., 1 vol. New York: Random, 1984.

Gresset, Michel. *A Faulkner Chronology*. Trans. Arthur B. Scharff. Jackson: UP of Mississippi, 1985.

BIBLIOGRAPHIES OF SECONDARY MATERIAL

American Literary Study, edited by various hands and published annually by Duke UP, provides a splendid summary of the previous year's work on all American authors, including Faulkner.

Bassett, John L. *William Faulkner: An Annotated Checklist of Criticism*. New York: David Lewis, 1972.

———. *Faulkner: An Annotated Checklist of Recent Criticism*. Kent: Kent State UP, 1983.

Jones, Diane Brown. *A Reader's Guide to the Short Stories of William Faulkner*. New York: G. K. Hall, 1994.

McHaney, Thomas L. *William Faulkner: A Reference Guide*. Boston: G. K. Hall, 1976.

Works of General Interest on William Faulkner

Editor's note: Criticism on the works of William Faulkner is far too vast an area to be able to do more here than merely suggest some of the more important places to go to do research on any aspect of his work. The following list is therefore highly selective. Researchers should also consult the bibliographies listed here for additional critical works.

Bleikasten, André. *The Ink of Melancholy*. Bloomington: Indiana UP, 1990.

Brooks, Cleanth. *William Faulkner: The Yoknapatawpha Country*. New Haven: Yale UP, 1963.

Carothers, James B. *William Faulkner's Short Stories*. Ann Arbor: U of Michigan P, 1985.

Ferguson, James. *Faulkner's Short Fiction*. Knoxville: U of Tennessee P, 1991.

Freud, Sigmund. *The Standard Edition of the Complete Psychological Works of Sigmund Freud*. Trans. and ed. James Strachey. London: The Hogarth Press and the Institute of Psycho-Analysis, 1955.

Gresset, Michel. *Fascination: Faulkner's Fiction, 1919–1936*. Durham: Duke UP, 1989.

Gwin, Minrose. *The Feminine and Faulkner: Reading (Beyond) Sexual Difference*. Knoxville: U of Tennessee P, 1989.

Irwin, John. *Doubling and Incest/Repetition and Revenge: A Speculative Reading of Faulkner*. Baltimore: Johns Hopkins UP, 1976.

Millgate, Michael. *The Achievement of William Faulkner*. New York: Random, 1966.

Polk, Noel. *Children of the Dark House: Text and Context in Faulkner.* Jackson: UP of Mississippi, 1996.

Roberts, Diane. *Faulkner and Southern Womanhood.* Athens: U of Georgia P, 1994.

Skei, Hans. *Bold and Tragical and Austere: William Faulkner's These 13: A Study.* Oslo: University of Oslo Department of Literature, 1977.

————. *William Faulkner: The Short Story Career.* Oslo: Universitetsforlaget, 1981.

————. *William Faulkner: The Novelist as Short Story Writer.* Oslo: Universitetsforlaget, 1985.

Critical Appraisals of "A Rose for Emily"

Note: As with the Works of General Interest, the following list is highly selective. Students and scholars at any level interested in "A Rose for Emily" should consult Diane Brown Jones's indispensable *A Reader's Guide to the Short Stories of William Faulkner,* listed earlier, and its bibliographical essay on "A Rose for Emily" (87–141).

Allen, Dennis W. "Horror and Perverse Delight: Faulkner's 'A Rose for Emily.'" *Modern Fiction Studies* 30 (1984): 685–96.

Arensberg, Mary, and Sara E. Schyfter. "Hairoglyphics in Faulkner's 'A Rose for Emily'/Reading the Primal Trace." *Boundary 2* 15 (1986–87): 123–34.

Barber, Marion. "The Two Emilys: A Ransom Suggestion to Faulkner?" *Notes on Mississippi Writers* 5 (1973): 103–05.

Barnes, Daniel R. "Faulkner's Miss Emily and Hawthorne's Old Maid." *Studies in Short Fiction* 9 (1972): 373–77.

Barth, Robert, Jr. "Faulkner and the Calvinist Tradition." *Thought* 39 (1964): 100–20.

Brooks, Cleanth. "A Note on Faulkner's Early Attempts at the Short Story." *Studies in Short Fiction* 10 (1973): 381–88.

————. "The Sense of Community in Yoknapatawpha Fiction." *The University of Mississippi Studies in English* 15 (1978): 3–18.

Brown, Suzanne Hunter. "'A Rose for Emily' by William Faulkner." *Short Story Theory at a Crossroads.* Ed. Susan Lohafer and Jo Ellen Clarey. Baton Rouge: LSU, 1989. 317–27.

Crosman, Robert. "How Readers Make Meaning." *College Literature* 9 (1982): 207–15.

Dillon, George L. "Styles of Reading." *Poetics Today* 3.2 (1982): 77–88.

Fetterley, Judith, "A Rose for 'A Rose for Emily.'" *The Resisting Reader: A Feminist Approach to American Literature.* Bloomington: Indiana UP, 1978. 34–45.

Garrison, Joseph M., Jr. "'Bought Flowers' in 'A Rose for Emily.'" *Studies in Short Fiction* 16 (1979): 341–44.

Heller, Terry. "The Telltale Hair: A Critical Study of William Faulkner's 'A Rose for Emily.'" *Arizona Quarterly* 28 (1972): 301–18.

Hendricks, William O. "'A Rose for Emily': A Syntagmatic Analysis." *PTL: A Journal for Descriptive Poetics and Theory of Literature* 2 (1997): 257–95.

Holland, Norman N. "Fantasy and Defense in Faulkner's 'A Rose for Emily.'" *Hartford Studies in Literature* 4 (1972): 1–35.

Inge, M. Thomas, ed. *A Rose for Emily*. Columbus, OH: Merrill, 1970.

Mellard, James M. "Faulkner's Miss Emily and Blake's 'Sick Rose': 'Invisible Worm,' *Nachträglichkeit*, and Retrospective Gothic." *The Faulkner Journal* 2 (1986): 37–45.

Moore, Gene E. "Of Time and Its Mathematical Progression: Problems of Chronology in Faulkner's 'A Rose for Emily.'" *Studies in Short Fiction* 29.2 (1992): 195–204.

Perry, Menakhem. "Literary Dynamics: How the Order of a Text Creates Its Meanings." *Poetics Today* 1 (1979): 35–64, 311–61.

Rodman, Isaac. "Irony and Isolation: Narrative Distance in Faulkner's 'A Rose for Emily.'" *The Faulkner Journal* 8 (1993): 3–12.

Scherting, Jack. "Emily Grierson's Oedipus Complex: Motif, Motive, and Meaning in Faulkner's 'A Rose for Emily.'" *Studies in Short Fiction* 17 (1980): 397–405.

Skinner, John L. "'A Rose for Emily': Against Interpretation." *Journal of Narrative Technique* 15 (1985): 42–51.

Stafford, T. J. "Tobe's Significance in 'A Rose for Emily.'" Inge, 87–89.

Sullivan, Ruth. "The Narrator in 'A Rose for Emily.'" *Journal of Narrative Technique* 1 (1971): 159–78.

West, Ray B., Jr. "Atmosphere and Theme in Faulkner's 'A Rose for Emily.'" *William Faulkner: Four Decades of Criticism.* Ed. Linda Welshimer Wagner. East Lansing: Michigan State UP, 1973. 192–98.

FILM ADAPTATION OF "A ROSE FOR EMILY"

A Rose for Emily. Screenplay by H. Kaye Dyal. Dir. Lyndon Chubbuck. Pyramid Films, 1982. Perf. Anjelica Huston.

WORLD WIDE WEB SITES

Padgett, John B. "William Faulkner: American Writer 1897–1962." Online posting. 12 May 1995. Chorus Networks. 10 Sept. 1999. <http://www.mcsr.olemiss.edu/~egjbp/faulkner/faulkner.html>.

"The William Faulkner Foundation, France." Online posting. 5 Dec. 1995. Chorus Networks. 11 Sept. 1999. <http://www.uhb.fr/Faulkner/>.

Easley, Larry. "The Center for Faulkner Studies." Online posting. 20 Aug. 1999. Chorus Networks. 11 Sept. 1999. <http://www2.semo.edu/cfs/homepage.html>.

Evans, David H. "The William Faulkner Society." Online posting. 25 Aug. 1999.
    Chorus Networks. 11 Sept. 1999. <http://www.utep.edu/mortimer/
    faulkner/mainfaulkner.htm>.
Shioya, Sachiko. "Faulkner's Page." Online posting. Nov. 1997. Chorus Networks.
    11 Sept. 1997. <http://www.asahi-net.or.jp/~BB8S-SOY/cont/
    faulkner/faulkm.html>.
Urgo, Joseph R. "Faulkner Discussion List." Bryant College.
    <majordomo@bryant.edu>.

Appendix:
Documenting Sources

A Guide to MLA
Documentation Style

Documentation is the acknowledgment of information from an outside source that you use in a paper. In general, give credit to your sources whenever you quote, paraphrase, summarize, or in any other way incorporate borrowed information or ideas into your work. Not to do so—on purpose or by accident—is to commit **plagiarism,** to appropriate the intellectual property of others. By following accepted conventions of documentation, you not only help avoid plagiarism, but also show your readers that you write with care and precision. In addition, you enable them to distinguish your ideas from those of your sources and, if they wish, to locate and consult the sources you cite.

Not all ideas from your sources need to be documented. You can assume that certain information—facts from encyclopedias, textbooks, newspapers, magazines, and dictionaries, or even from television and radio—is common knowledge. Even if the information is new to you, it need not be documented as long as it is found in several reference sources and as long as you do not use the exact wording of your source. Information that is in dispute or that is the original contribution of a particular person, however, *must* be documented. You need not, for example, document the fact that Arthur Miller's *Death of a Salesman* was first performed in 1949 or that it won a Pulitzer Prize for drama. (You could find this information in any current encyclopedia.) You would, however, have to document a critic's interpretation of a performance or a scholar's analysis of an early draft of the play, even if you do not use your source's exact words.

Students of literature use the documentation style recommended by the Modern Language Association of America (MLA), a professional organization of teachers and students of English and other languages. This method of documentation, the one that you should use any time you write a literature paper, has three components: *parenthetical references in the text, a list of works cited,* and *sometimes explanatory notes.*

Parenthetical References in the Text

MLA documentation uses references inserted in parentheses within the text that refer to an alphabetical list of works cited at the end of the paper. A typical **parenthetical reference** consists of the author's last name and a page number.

> Gwendolyn Brooks uses the sonnet form to create poems that have a wide social and aesthetic range (Williams 972).

If you use more than one source by the same author, include a shortened title in the parenthetical reference. In the following entry, "Brooks's Way" is a shortened form of the complete title of the article "Gwendolyn Brooks's Way with the Sonnet."

> Brooks not only knows Shakespeare, Spenser, and Milton, but she also knows the full range of African-American poetry (Williams, "Brooks's Way" 972).

If you mention the author's name or the title of the work in your paper, only a page reference is necessary.

> According to Gladys Margaret Williams in "Gwendolyn Brooks's Way with the Sonnet," Brooks combines a sensitivity to poetic forms with a depth of emotion appropriate for her subject matter (972-73).

Keep in mind that you use different punctuation for parenthetical references used with *paraphrases and summaries,* with *direct quotations run in with the text,* and with *quotations of more than four lines.*

Paraphrases and Summaries

Place the parenthetical reference after the last word of the sentence and before the final punctuation:

> In her works Brooks combines the pessimism of modernist poetry with the optimism of the Harlem Renaissance (Smith 978).

Direct quotations run in with the text

Place the parenthetical reference after the quotation marks and before the final punctuation:

> According to Gary Smith, Brooks's <u>A Street in Bronzeville</u> "conveys the primacy of suffering in the lives of poor Black women" (980).

> According to Gary Smith, the poems in <u>A Street in Bronzeville</u> "served notice that Brooks had learned her craft [. . .]" (978).

> Along with Thompson we must ask, "Why did it take so long for critics to acknowledge that Gwendolyn Brooks is an important voice in twentieth-century American poetry?" (123)

Quotations set off from the text

Double-space above and below the quotation, as well as within the quotation. Quotations of more than four lines are indented ten spaces (or one inch) from the margin and are not enclosed within quotation marks. The first line of a single paragraph of quoted material is not indented further. If you quote two or more paragraphs, indent the first line of each paragraph three additional spaces (one-quarter inch).

Omit the quotation marks and place the parenthetical reference one space after the final punctuation.

> For Gary Smith, the identity of Brooks's African-American women is inextricably linked with their sense of race and poverty:
>
> > For Brooks, unlike the Renaissance poets, the victimization of poor Black women becomes not simply a minor chord but a predominant theme of <u>A Street in Bronzeville</u>. Few, if any, of her female characters are able to free themselves from a web of poverty that threatens to strangle their lives. (980)

SAMPLE REFERENCES

The following formats are used for parenthetical references to various kinds of sources used in papers about literature. Keep in mind that the parenthetical reference contains just enough information to enable readers to find the source in the list of works cited at the end of the paper.

An entire work

August Wilson's play <u>Fences</u> treats many themes frequently expressed in modern drama.

[When citing an entire work, state the name of the author in your paper instead of in a parenthetical reference.]

A work by two or three authors

Myths cut across boundaries and cultural spheres and reappear in strikingly similar forms from country to country (Feldman and Richardson 124).

The effect of a work of literature depends on the audience's predispositions that derive from membership in various social groups (Hovland, Janis, and Kelley 87).

A work by more than three authors

Hawthorne's short stories frequently use a combination of allegorical and symbolic methods (Guerin et al. 91).

[The abbreviation *et al.* is Latin for "and others."]

A work in an anthology

In his essay "Flat and Round Characters" E. M. Forster distinguishes between one-dimensional characters and those that are well developed (Stevick 223-31).

[The parenthetical reference cites the anthology (edited by Stevick) that contains Forster's essay; full information about the anthology appears in the list of works cited.]

A work with volume and page numbers

In 1961, one of Albee's plays, <u>The Zoo Story</u>, was
finally performed in America (Eagleton 2:17).

An indirect source

Wagner observed that myth and history stood before
him "with opposing claims" (qtd. in Winkler 10).

[The abbreviation *qtd. in* (quoted in) indicates that the quoted material is
not taken from the original source.]

A play or poem with numbered lines

"Give thy thoughts no tongue," says Polonius,
"Nor any unproportioned thought his act"
(<u>Ham</u>. 1.3.59-60).

[The parentheses contain the act, scene, and line numbers, separated by periods. When included in parenthetical references, titles of the books of the
Bible and well-known literary works are often abbreviated—*Gen.* for *Gen-
esis* and *Ado* for *Much Ado about Nothing*, for example.]

"I muse my life-long hate, and without flinch / I
bear it nobly as I live my part," says Claude McKay
in his bitterly ironic poem "The White City" (3-4).

[Notice that a slash [/] is used to separate two or three lines of poetry run in
with the text. The parenthetical reference cites the lines quoted. More than
three lines of poetry should be set off like a long prose passage. For special
emphasis, fewer lines may also be set off in this manner. Punctuation, spelling, and capitalization, and indentation are reproduced *exactly*.]

The List of Works Cited

Parenthetical references refer to a **list of works cited** that includes all the
sources you refer to in your paper. (If your list includes all the works consulted, whether you cite them or not, use the title *Works Consulted*.) Begin
the works cited list on a new page, continuing the page numbers of the

paper. For example, if the text of the paper ends on page 6, the works cited section will begin on page 7.

Center the title *Works Cited* one inch from the top of the page. Arrange entries alphabetically, according to the last name of each author (or the first word of the title if the author is unknown). Articles—*a, an,* and *the*—at the beginning of a title are not considered first words. Thus *A Handbook of Critical Approaches to Literature* would be alphabetized under *H.* In order to conserve space, publishers' names are abbreviated—for example, *Harcourt* for Harcourt College Publishers. Double-space the entire Works Cited list between and within entries. Begin typing each entry at the left margin, and indent subsequent lines five spaces or one-half inch. The entry itself generally has three divisions—author, title, and publishing information— separated by periods.*

A book by a single author

    Kingston, Maxine Hong. The Woman Warrior: Memoirs of
        a Girlhood among Ghosts. New York: Knopf, 1976.

A book by two or three authors

    Feldman, Burton, and Robert D. Richardson. The Rise
        of Modern Mythology. Bloomington: Indiana UP,
        1972.

Notice that only the *first* author's name is in reverse order.

A book by more than three authors

    Guerin, Wilfred, et al., eds. A Handbook of Critical
        Approaches to Literature. 3rd ed. New York:
        Harper, 1992.

[Instead of using *et al.,* you may list all the authors' names in the order in which they appear on the title page.]

---

* The fifth edition of the MLA Handbook for Writers of Research Papers (1999) shows a single space after all end punctuation.

Two or more works by the same author

> Novoa, Juan-Bruce. <u>Chicano Authors: Inquiry by In-</u>
> <u>terview</u>, Austin: U of Texas P, 1980.
> ---. "Themes in Rudolfo Anaya's Work." Address
> given at New Mexico State University, Las
> Cruces. 11 Apr. 1987.

[List two or more works by the same author in alphabetical order by title. Include the author's full name in the first entry; use three unspaced hyphens followed by a period to take the place of the author's name in second and subsequent entries.]

An edited book

> Oosthuizen, Ann, ed. <u>Sometimes When It Rains: Writ-</u>
> <u>ings by South African Women</u>. New York: Pandora,
> 1987.

[Note that the abbreviation *ed.* stands for *editor.* If there is more than one editor, use *eds.*]

A book with a volume number

> Eagleton, T. Allston. <u>A History of the New York</u>
> <u>Stage</u>. Vol. 2. Englewood Cliffs: Prentice,
> 1987.

[All three volumes have the same title.]

> Durant, Will, and Ariel Durant. <u>The Age of Napoleon:</u>
> <u>A History of European Civilization from 1789 to</u>
> <u>1815</u>. New York: Simon, 1975.

[Each volume has a different title, so you may cite an individual book without referring to the other volumes.]

A short story, poem, or play in a collection of the author's work

> Gordimer, Nadine. "Once upon a Time." <u>"Jump" and</u>
> <u>Other Stories</u>. New York: Farrar, 1991. 23-30.

A short story in an anthology

> Salinas, Marta. "The Scholarship Jacket." <u>Nosotros:</u>
> <u>Latina Literature Today</u>. Ed. Maria del Carmen
> Boza, Beverly Silva, and Carmen Valle. Bingham-
> ton: Bilingual, 1986. 68-70.

[The inclusive page numbers follow the year of publication. Note that here the abbreviation *Ed.* stands for *Edited by*.]

A poem in an anthology

> Simmerman, Jim. "Child's Grave, Hale County, Ala-
> bama." <u>The Pushcart Prize, X: Best of the Small</u>
> <u>Presses</u>. Ed. Bill Henderson. New York: Penguin,
> 1986. 198-99.

A play in an anthology

> Hughes, Langston. <u>Mother and Child</u>. <u>Black Drama An-</u>
> <u>thology</u>. Ed. Woodie King and Ron Miller. New
> York: NAL, 1986. 399-406.

An article in an anthology

> Forster, E. M. "Flat and Round Characters." <u>The The-</u>
> <u>ory of the Novel</u>. Ed. Philip Stevick. New York:
> Free, 1980. 223-31.

More than one selection from the same anthology

If you are using more than one selection from an anthology, cite the anthology in one entry. In addition, list each individual selection separately, including the author and title of the selection, the anthology editor's last name, and the inclusive page numbers.

> Kirszner, Laurie G., and Stephen R. Mandell, eds.
> <u>Literature: Reading, Reacting, Writing</u>. 3rd ed.
> Fort Worth: Harcourt, 1997.
> Rich, Adrienne. "Diving into the Wreck." Kirszner
> and Mandell 874-76.

A translation

Carpentier, Alejo. <u>Reasons of State</u>. Trans. Francis
Partridge. New York: Norton, 1976.

An article in a journal with continuous pagination in each issue

Le Guin, Ursula K. "American Science Fiction and the
Other." <u>Science Fiction Studies</u> 2 (1975):
208-10.

An article with separate pagination in each issue

Grossman, Robert. "The Grotesque in Faulkner's
'A Rose for Emily.'" <u>Mosaic</u> 20.3 (1987): 40-55.

20.3 signifies volume 20, issue 3.

An article in a magazine

Milosz, Czeslaw. "A Lecture." <u>New Yorker</u> 22 June
1992: 32.
"Solzhenitsyn: An Artist Becomes an Exile." <u>Time</u>
25 Feb. 1974: 34+.

[34+ indicates that the article appears on pages that are not consecutive; in
this case the article begins on page 34 and then continues on page 37. An
article with no listed author is entered by title on the Works Cited list.]

An article in a daily newspaper

Oates, Joyce Carol. "When Characters from the Page
Are Made Flesh on the Screen." <u>New York Times</u>
23 Mar. 1986, late ed.: C1+.

[C1+ indicates that the article begins on page 1 of Section C and continues
on a subsequent page.]

An article in a reference book

"Dance Theatre of Harlem." <u>The New Encyclopaedia
Britannica: Micropaedia</u>. 15th ed. 1987.

[You do not need to include publication information for well-known reference books.]

> Grimstead, David. "Fuller, Margaret Sarah." <u>Encyclopedia of American Biography</u>. Ed. John A. Garraty. New York: Harper, 1974.

[You must include publication information when citing reference books that are not well known.]

A CD-ROM: Entry with a print version

> Zurbach, Kate. "The Linguistic Roots of Three Terms." <u>Linguistic Quarterly</u> 37 (1994): 12-47. <u>Infotrac: Magazine Index Plus</u>. CD-ROM. Information Access. Jan. 1996.

[When you cite information with a print version from a CD-ROM, include the publication information, the underlined title of the database (<u>Infotrac: Magazine Index Plus</u>), the publication medium (CD-ROM), the name of the company that produced the CD-ROM (Information Access), and the electronic publication date.]

A CD-ROM: Entry with no print version

> "Surrealism." <u>Encarta 1999</u>. CD-ROM. Redmond: Microsoft, 1999.

[If you are citing a part of a work, include the title in quotation marks.]

> <u>A Music Lover's Multimedia Guide to Beethoven's 5th</u>. CD-ROM. Spring Valley: Interactive, 1993.

[If you are citing an entire work, include the underlined title.]

An online source: Entry with a print version

> Dekoven, Marianne. "Utopias Limited: Post-sixties and Postmodern American Fiction." <u>Modern Fiction Studies</u> 41.1 (Spring 1995): 121-34. 17 Mar. 1996 <http://muse.jhu.edu/journals/ MFS/v041/41.1 dekoven.html>.

When you cite information with a print version from an online source, include the publication information for the printed source, the number of pages or number of paragraphs (if available), and the date of access. Be sure to include the electronic address (URL) in angle brackets.

Sometimes, you may use a commercial online service (America Online or Lexis/Nexis, for example) where you use a keyword, not an electronic address, to retrieve information. If you use a keyword to retrieve information, end your citation by typing *Keyword* followed by a colon and the word itself.

> "Gunpowder." <u>Compton's Encyclopedia Online</u>. Vers.
> 2.0. 1999. America Online. 28 Aug. 1999. Key-
> word: Compton's.

If, instead of a keyword, you use a series of topics to find your material, type *Path* followed by the topics (separated by semicolons) you used to locate your material.

> O'Hara, Sandra. "Reexamining the Canon." <u>Time</u> 12 May
> 1994: 27. America Online. 22 Aug. 1994. Path:
> Education; Literature; <u>Time</u>.

An online source: Public Posting

> Peters, Olaf. "Studying English through German."
> Online posting. 29 Feb. 1996. Foreign Language
> Forum, Multi Language Section. CompuServe.
> 15 Mar. 1996.
> Gilford, Mary. "Dog Heroes in Children's Litera-
> ture." Online posting. 4 Oct. 1996. 23 Mar.
> 1996.<News:alt.animals.dogs>. America Online.

[**WARNING:** Using information from online forums and newsgroups is risky. Contributors are not necessarily experts, and frequently they are incorrect and misinformed. Unless you can be certain the information you are receiving from these sources is reliable, do not use it in your papers.]

An online source: Electronic Text

> Twain, Mark. <u>Adventures of Huckleberry Finn</u>. From
> <u>The Writing of Mark Twain</u>. Vol. 13. New York:
> Harper, 1970. <u>Wiretap.spies</u>. 13 Jan. 1996

```
<http.//www.sci.dixie.edu/DixieCollege/Ebooks/
huckfin.html>.
```

This electronic text was originally published by Harper. The name of the repository for the electronic edition is Wiretap.spies (underlined).

An online source: E-mail

```
Adkins, Camille. E-mail to the author. 8 June 1995.
```

An interview

```
Brooks, Gwendolyn. "Interviews." Triquarterly 60
    (1984): 405-10.
```

A lecture or address

```
Novoa, Juan-Bruce. "Themes in Rudolfo Anaya's Work."
    New Mexico State University, Las Cruces,
    11 Apr. 1987.
```

A film or videocassette

```
"A Worn Path." By Eudora Welty. Dir. John Reid and
    Claudia Velasco. Perf. Cora Lee Day and Con-
    chita Ferrell. Videocassette. Harcourt, 1994.
```

In addition to the title, the director, and the year, include other pertinent information such as the principal performers.

Explanatory Notes

Explanatory notes, indicated by a superscript (a raised number) in the text, may be used to cite several sources at once or to provide commentary or explanations that do not fit smoothly into your paper. The full text of these notes appears on the first numbered page following the last page of the paper. (If your paper has no explanatory notes, the Works Cited page follows the last page of the paper.) Like Works Cited entries, explanatory notes are double spaced within and between entries. However, the first line of each explanatory note is indented five spaces (or one-half inch), with subsequent lines flush with the left-hand margin.

TO CITE SEVERAL SOURCES

In the paper

> Surprising as it may seem, there have been many attempts to define literature.[1]

In the note

> [1] For an overview of critical opinion, see Arnold 72; Eagleton 1-2; Howe 43-44; and Abrams 232-34.

TO PROVIDE EXPLANATIONS

In the paper

> In recent years Gothic novels have achieved great popularity.[3]

In the note

> [3] Gothic novels, works written in imitation of medieval romances, originally relied on supernatural occurrences. They flourished in the late eighteenth and early nineteenth centuries.

Credits

Helter, Terry
"The Telltale Hair: A Critical Study of William Faulkner's 'A Rose for Emily.'"
Arizona Quarterly 28 (1972). Reprinted by permission of the Regents of the
University of Arizona.

Moore, Gene M.
"Of Time and Its Mathematical Progression: Problems of Chronology in Faulkner's 'A Rose for Emily.'" *Studies in Short Fiction* 29 (1992):195–204. Copyright
©1992 by Newberry College. Reprinted by permission.

Rodman, Isaac
"Irony and Isolation: Narrative Distance in Faulkner's 'A Rose for Emily.'" *The
Faulkner Journal* VIII: 2 (Spring 1993). Copyright © 1993 by The University
of Akron. Reprinted by permission of the author and the University of Central
Florida. The Faulkner Journal, Department of English, University of Central
Florida, P.O. Box 161346, Orlando, FL32816-1346.

Scherting, Jack
"Emily Grierson's Oedipus Complex: Motif, Motive, and Meaning in Faulkner's
'A Rose for Emily.'" *Studies in Short Fiction* 17 (1980): 397–405. Copyright ©
1980 by Newberry College. Reprinted by permission.

Sullivan, Ruth
"The Narrator in 'A Rose for Emily.'" *The Journal of Narrative Technique* Vol. 1,
No. 3 (September 1971): 159–178. Reproduced by permission of the publisher
and the author.